Emerson, Thoreau, and the Transcendentalist Movement
Part II

Professor Ashton Nichols

THE TEACHING COMPANY ®

PUBLISHED BY:

THE TEACHING COMPANY
4151 Lafayette Center Drive, Suite 100
Chantilly, Virginia 20151-1232
1-800-TEACH-12
Fax—703-378-3819
www.teach12.com

ISBN 1-59803-244-5

Ashton Nichols, Ph.D.

John and Ann Conser Curley Professor of English, Dickinson College

Professor Ashton Nichols was born in Washington, D.C.; grew up in Baltimore, Maryland; and graduated in 1975 from the University of Virginia with a Bachelor of Arts degree with high honors in philosophy. As an undergraduate, he was a DuPont Scholar and a member of Phi Beta Kappa. He pursued a career in journalism, first at the *Free-Lance Star* in Fredericksburg, Virginia, where he received awards from the Associated Press and the Virginia Press Association, and later, at the National Trust for Historic Preservation in Washington, D.C. In 1978, he returned to the University of Virginia, receiving his M.A. in English in 1979 and his Ph.D. in English in 1984.

In 1988, after four years of teaching at Auburn University, Dr. Nichols was appointed assistant professor of English at Dickinson College. His first book appeared that year, *The Poetics of Epiphany: 19ᵗʰ-Century Origins of the Modern Literary Moment* (University of Alabama). He was promoted to associate professor in 1992 and to full professor in 1998. In 2003, he was named the John J. Curley '60 and Ann Conser Curley '63 Faculty Professor of Language and Literature in the English Department at Dickinson. His research and teaching focus on the relationship between 19ᵗʰ- and 20ᵗʰ-century literature and, more recently, on connections between literature, particularly poetry, and science during the century before Charles Darwin's *Origin of Species*.

Dr. Nichols published *The Revolutionary "I": Wordsworth and the Politics of Self-Presentation* (London: Macmillan; New York: St. Martin's) in 1998, and most recently, he has edited a teaching anthology, *Romantic Natural Histories: William Wordsworth, Charles Darwin, and Others*, for Houghton Mifflin in Boston (2004). He has also produced *A Romantic Natural History: 1750–1859*, a hypertext scholarly project that has been recognized for excellence by *The New York Times* and the BBC in London. His scholarly publications cover a wide range of topics: Chinua Achebe, Derek Walcott, Thomas Pynchon, Seamus Heaney, African exploration narratives, Victorian poetry, and travel writing. Dr. Nichols has also published nature writing essays, numerous poems, and several short stories. His awards include the Lindback Award for Distinguished Teaching and the Ganoe Award for Inspirational Teaching. In recent years, he has delivered keynote addresses and invited lectures in China, England, Italy, Japan, Portugal, Cameroon, and Morocco.

Grants to support Dr. Nichols's scholarship and teaching have been provided by the National Endowment for the Humanities and the Mellon Foundation. He is listed in *Who's Who in America* for 2000 and *Who's Who in the World* for 2001. Dr. Nichols is a member of the Modern Language Association, the North American Society for the Study of Romanticism, the Association for the Study of Literature and Environment, the William Morris Society, the 19th-Century Studies Association, and the American Conference on Romanticism. He lives in Carlisle, Pennsylvania, with his wife Kimberley, with whom he has four grown daughters.

Table of Contents
Emerson, Thoreau, and the
Transcendentalist Movement
Part II

Publication Credits:

Professor Nichols quotes primary-source text excerpts and matters of
fact from the following Web sites:

- *American Transcendentalism Web*. Ann Woodlief et al.
  Virginia Commonwealth University.
  www.vcu.edu/engweb/transcendentalism/.

- *Dictionary of Unitarian and Universalist Biography*.
  Unitarian Universalist Historical Society (UUHS).
  uua.org/uuhs/duub/.

©2006 The Teaching Company Limited Partnership

Emerson, Thoreau, and the Transcendentalist Movement

Scope:

Few movements in American social and intellectual history have been as influential as the cluster of ideas we have come to call Transcendentalism. From Ralph Waldo Emerson's "self-reliant soul" and Henry David Thoreau's "different drummer" to modern ideas about individualism and democracy, Transcendentalism has had a powerful impact on central aspects of American life. In addition to familiar names, such as Emily Dickinson and Frederick Douglass, this series of lectures will examine a number of less well-known American originals: Margaret Fuller, William Ellery Channing, A. Bronson Alcott, and Jones Very. After exploring the religious dimensions of this wide-ranging movement, as well as its contributions to American politics and society, these lectures will end with reflections on the impact of Transcendentalism on contemporary American and world culture.

Our course will begin with the life and career of Ralph Waldo Emerson, the single most important figure behind American Transcendentalism. We will then move to a careful examination of Henry David Thoreau, Emerson's most influential disciple. From Emerson's contention that divinity resides in every person to Thoreau's defense of civil disobedience, we will examine the details of Transcendentalism, the powerful intellectual movement these two helped to found and foster. After our study of the two figures at the heart of the movement, we will explore a wide range of engaging individuals: educational activists, such as Bronson Alcott and Elizabeth Peabody; literary figures, including Walt Whitman and Emily Dickinson; and social reformers, such as Theodore Parker and Moncure Conway. Many of these teachers, writers, and thinkers were calling for nothing less than a remaking of society: the abolition of slavery, equal rights for women, freedom of religious thought and practice, educational reform, and attention to those aspects of experience that were essential to a good life. It is hard for us now to appreciate how radical and revolutionary Transcendentalism seemed in the decades leading up to the Civil War. These ideas, however, contributed to reforms and ways of thinking that are still with us today.

By tracing these wide-ranging currents of thought, we will come to understand ideas that led to other social changes, such as the development of liberal theologies, the rise of the periodical press, and numerous utopian and religious experiments. Our lectures will engage major texts, including Emerson's *Nature* and "Self-Reliance," Thoreau's *Walden*, Fuller's *Woman in the Nineteenth Century*, and Whitman's *Leaves of Grass*. We will also confront crucial historical events: John Brown's raid, the Civil War, the rise of industrial New England, and the decline of the agricultural South. Our concluding lectures will identify Transcendentalism as a movement that not only shaped the 19th century but also continues to have a powerful influence on our own era. From the passive resistance of Mahatma Gandhi and Martin Luther King, Jr., to increased gender equality, from the role of liberal denominations in American religion to emphasis on global understanding and cooperation, Transcendentalism continues to shape a uniquely American way of viewing ourselves and our place in the wider world.

Lecture Thirteen
Margaret Fuller and Rights for Women

Scope:

From Louisa May Alcott, we turn to another woman whose name became synonymous with several of the main currents of Transcendentalism. Margaret Fuller learned Latin and Greek at an early age and was translating Goethe by the time she took over the education of her siblings upon their father's early death. She served as a teacher at Bronson Alcott's Temple School, then as a magazine writer and as the first editor of *The Dial* magazine. After Horace Greeley asked her to work as a reviewer for the *New York Tribune*, she became a foreign correspondent. Her groundbreaking publications included "The Great Lawsuit: Man versus Men, Woman versus Women," which was revised as *Woman in the Nineteenth Century*, the major work in which she argued unequivocally for equal rights for women. Tragically, she drowned, along with her Italian husband and their son, in sight of Fire Island, New York, upon her return to America at the age of 40. Thoreau was dispatched to find her manuscript writings, but he reported finding only unidentifiable human remains on the beach.

Outline

I. Margaret Fuller (1810–1850) was a pioneer of women's rights in thought and practice.

   A. Consider first the position of women in the middle of 19th-century America.

      1. They could not vote and had no significant political rights or role of any kind.

      2. A woman in Massachusetts could not own private property distinct from her husband until 1854.

      3. Divorce was almost unheard of, and in the very few cases where a divorce was granted, men usually kept rights over property and children.

      4. Women had virtually no access to higher education or advanced professional education.

      5. Manual factory labor, domestic work, and teaching were their only acceptable occupations.

6. A woman, regardless of her position in society, was expected to have her life determined solely by men and her relationships with men.

B. Margaret Fuller spent her adult life advocating the idea that women's lives might not have to be shaped entirely by the lives of the men around them.

    1. Her own life had been dramatically altered by the death of her father when she was a young adult, leaving her largely responsible for the emotional and economic welfare of her family.

    2. She argued that women needed the freedom to grow and develop through education, reading, conversation, friendship.

    3. She claimed that marriage required radical reform to make it more like a "meeting of the souls"; as it stood, it was merely "convenience and utility" designed so that women might "find a protector, and a home."

    4. These ideas hearken back to Mary Wollstonecraft and earlier English feminists, but they have a particularly American stamp: female liberty, democracy for all.

    5. "By Man I mean both man and woman; these are the two halves of one thought. I lay no especial stress on the welfare of either. I believe that the development of the one cannot be effected without that of the other. My highest wish is that this truth should be distinctly and rationally apprehended, and the condition of life and freedom recognized as the same for the daughters and the sons of time; twin exponents of a divine thought" ("Preface" to *Woman in the Nineteenth Century*, 1845).

C. Fuller was powerfully influenced by Emerson and other Transcendentalists, but she found herself influencing men's thinking, as well.

    1. Emerson invited her to join meetings of the Transcendentalist circle by 1838.

    2. Within a year, when it came time to select a first editor for *The Dial*, Fuller was chosen by Emerson and soon found herself writing large portions of the influential journal in her own words, as well as corresponding with, and editing the works of, Emerson himself, Thoreau, Alcott, Channing, and others.

3. Emerson said of her, "She was an active, inspiring companion and correspondent, and all the art, the thought, the nobleness in New England seemed at that moment [the 1830s] related to her and she to it."

4. Emerson's lecture entitled "Woman," which he delivered to the Women's Rights Convention in Boston in 1855, is clearly a result of her influence on him. *Woman in the Nineteenth Century* had been published a decade earlier.

D. Fuller was sufficiently forward looking, and frank enough, to link the topic of sexuality to women's rights but also to men's rights.

1. She argued for the need to re-imagine what we would now call gender roles; she argued, "there is no wholly masculine man," but also, "no purely feminine woman."

2. She was influenced by the Polish writer Adam Mickiewicz, a poet of romantic, if sometimes illicit, love.

3. She met and admired George Sand, the cross-dressing female novelist, notorious for her combination of social activism and sexual promiscuity.

4. Fuller was, to some, also a version of the scandalous scarlet woman, whose sexual freedom led to an illegitimate child and a Fourierist, or "natural," marriage to her Italian lover, d'Ossoli, then 10 years her junior.

5. She alienated some people because of a personality that was variously described as strident, energetic, and intense. Nathaniel Hawthorne and James Russell Lowell both caricatured her in print, while Sophia Peabody Hawthorne referred to her as "Queen Margaret."

II. Fuller's life consistently embodied her ideals.

A. She was extremely precocious as a child, learning Latin and many other subjects from her demanding father.

1. She began her career as a schoolteacher at Bronson Alcott's Temple School and the Green Street School in Providence, Rhode Island.

2. After two years, uncharacteristically for women of her time, she quit teaching, claiming that she needed more time for her own writing.

B. Fuller's most original and influential professional activities were her organized "Conversations" for women.

    1. From 1839 to 1844, she held her series of these "Conversations" in Boston, where she encouraged women to gather to think and talk about ideas. It is now hard for us to appreciate the radical nature of this idea.

    2. She was, however, following in the footsteps of Elizabeth Palmer Peabody's "reading parties" and was influenced by Bronson Alcott's idea for similar coed conversations.

    3. Fuller's friend Sophia Dana Ripley, wife of George Ripley and cofounder with him of Brook Farm, helped to gather together women for conversation around such topics as "What were we born to do? How shall we do it?"

    4. The actual meeting place was the parlor of Elizabeth Palmer Peabody's home. Approximately two dozen women appeared for the first meeting, and many other women soon found a new intellectual outlet here.

C. These dialogues led Fuller directly to her most influential work, *Woman in the Nineteenth Century*.

    1. Fuller published "The Great Lawsuit: Man versus Men and Woman versus Women" in *The Dial* in July of 1843, shortly after Emerson had replaced her as editor.

    2. The essay was revised and appeared as *Woman in the Nineteenth Century* in February 1845, a volume that argued for the end of women's subordination and a new view of their lives as free individuals.

    3. Her logic is clear and concise: Even liberal men are often hypocrites because they advocate racial freedom while still restricting women's rights; likewise, these same men say that women are physically and emotionally unable to assume responsible positions in civic life, but they are appropriate for rigorous farm work, as well as the most important task in any society, the raising and educating of young children.

    4. Fuller linked "the woman question," then being hotly debated in England as well as America, directly to Emersonian self-reliance: "What Woman needs is not as a woman to act or rule," she wrote, "but as a nature to grow, as an intellect to discern, as a soul to live freely and unimpeded, to unfold such powers as were given her when we left our common home."

5. She did not ignore men. In fact, she praised earlier writers, such as Shelley, Wordsworth, and Byron, for their understanding and sympathetic depictions of women and women's situation in their works.

D. Fuller traveled on a tour of the Great Lakes with her friend Sarah Freeman Clarke and produced *Summer on the Lakes, in 1843.*

1. The book was so well written and offered such an insightful analysis of the American Midwest at the time, that the famous newspaper editor Horace Greeley invited Fuller to begin work as a book reviewer and review editor for the *New York Tribune*. She flourished in this task and soon moved into an expanded role as a commentator on art and the wider culture.

2. By 1846, Greeley had invited Fuller to become a foreign correspondent, one of the first such journalists in America and certainly one of the first women. In Europe, she soon met and befriended the likes of Thomas Carlyle, George Sand, and numerous artists, intellectuals, and politicians.

3. She arrived in Italy in 1847, where she met and fell in love with the Marquis Giovanni Angelo d'Ossoli and gave birth to an illegitimate son; the two may have married later.

4. During the siege of Rome by the French in 1849, Fuller showed her practical side by assuming a leadership role in a Roman hospital. Meanwhile, her husband was fighting actively as an Italian partisan.

5. She also met Giuseppe Mazzini, the Italian patriot whose socialism resonated with her own political ideals. When the Italian cause collapsed, however, she decided to return to America.

E. Fuller became as famous in death as in life because of the circumstances of her drowning at age 40.

1. She sailed from Europe to America with d'Ossoli and their son in May 1850.

2. The ship's captain died on the journey; an inexperienced sailor took over.
3. The ship went down in a terrible storm in sight of Fire Island, New York.
4. Emerson sent Thoreau to recover her manuscripts from the wreckage, but he reported finding only unidentifiable human remains on the beach.

III. Fuller's influence has been variable over time but extensive.

    A. By 1881, suffragettes Susan B. Anthony and Elizabeth Cady Stanton could claim that Fuller "possessed more influence on the thought of American women than any woman previous to her time."

        1. She contributed significantly to the American Renaissance in literature and to various 19th-century reform movements.
        2. She was described as brilliant. She intellectually challenged the likes of Emerson and other male thinkers.
        3. Women who attended her conversations, like many men of the time, described her influence as life-altering, rather like modern consciousness-raising or self-help sessions.

    B. Fuller's major work, *Woman in the Nineteenth Century*, had a direct influence on the women's rights movement.

        1. "I think women need, especially at this juncture, a much greater range of occupation than they have, to rouse their latent powers."
        2. The book is now considered a classic of feminist thought in America. Its influence was powerfully felt as early as the gathering of women's rights advocates in Seneca Falls, New York, only three years after its publication.
        3. By putting her principles into action in her own life in what were seen as extreme ways, however, Fuller alienated many.

    C. Her influence was affected by those who sought to criticize her, as well as by those who tried to protect her reputation.

        1. Hawthorne described her as a "great humbug." His character Zenobia in *The Blithedale Romance*, his satirical novel about Brook Farm, is based on Fuller.

2. Later editors, such as William Henry Channing and James Freeman Clarke, worked to soften the intensity of Fuller's thought. In *Memoirs of Margaret Fuller Ossoli* (1852), they rewrote passages from her correspondence and struck offensive sections from her journals.
3. By the 1960s, the modern women's movement had revived intense interest in Fuller's life and work; a great deal of scholarship has appeared since then.
4. She is now taught in many college and university classes, and there is an active scholarly society dedicated to the study of her work and influence.

Essential Reading:

Fuller, Margaret. *The Essential Margaret Fuller*. Ed. Jeffrey Steele.

Dickenson, Donna. *Margaret Fuller: Writing a Woman's Life*.

Supplementary Reading:

Zwarg, Christina. *Feminist Conversations: Fuller, Emerson, and the Play of Reading*.

Questions to Consider:

1. Why were women central to American Transcendentalism from its earliest beginnings?
2. How does Margaret Fuller's career parallel the aspirations of many women from her own time to the present day?

Lecture Thirteen—Transcript
Margaret Fuller and Rights for Women

From Louisa May Alcott, we turn to another woman whose name became synonymous with several of the main currents of Transcendentalist thought. Margaret Fuller had learned Latin and Greek at an early age and was translating the German poet, Goethe, by the time she took over the education of all of her siblings upon their father's early death. She served as a head teacher at Bronson Alcott's Temple School, then later as a magazine writer, and as the first editor of the influential *The Dial* magazine.

After the newspaperman, Horace Greeley, asked her to work as a reviewer for his *New York Tribune*, she went on to become a foreign correspondent, a remarkable achievement for a woman of that era. Her groundbreaking publications included: "The Great Lawsuit: Man Versus Men, Woman Versus Women," which was revised as *Woman in the Nineteenth Century,* her major work, in which she argued insistently and unequivocally for equal rights for all women. She drowned, quite tragically, along with her Italian husband and their son while in sight of Fire Island, New York, upon her return from Europe to America at the age of only 40. Henry David Thoreau was dispatched to find her remaining manuscript writings, but he reported that he was only able to find unidentifiable human remains among the ship timbers on the beach.

Fuller was one of the most influential pioneers of women's rights in thought and in practice in 19th-century America. Let us consider first, by way of introduction, the position of women in the middle of the 19th century in the United States. They could not vote, and they had no significant political rights or political role of any kind. A woman in Massachusetts could not even own property, as distinct from her husband's property, until 1854. Divorce at this time, no matter how terrible the marriage, was almost unheard of and in those very few cases, when a divorce might be granted, it was men who usually kept rights over property and even over the children—almost the reverse of our own current situation.

Women had virtually no access to higher education or to advanced professional degrees in any field. In fact, there were really only three acceptable occupations for women; they could work as manual factory laborers, and of course, that had class connotations that we will discuss later; it was acceptable for them to be teachers; but clearly their most common work was the domestic labor that they performed in their own households.

To summarize, a woman, regardless of her position in society—by that I mean regardless of the class from which she came—was expected to have her life determined solely by men and also by her relationships with men, starting with her father, proceeding to her husband and perhaps her brothers or uncles, depending on her familial situation.

With that information by way of introduction, we can see how significant it must have been for Margaret Fuller to spend her adult life advocating the idea that women's lives might not have to be shaped entirely by the lives of the men around them, but that they might have their own independent authority to make decisions that would affect them.

Fuller's own life had been dramatically altered by the death of her father, as was so often the case at this time in history, while she was still a young adult, an event that left her largely responsible for the emotional and also for the economic welfare of her family. As a result—not only of this circumstance, but also her own observations of the lives of women around her—she argued that women needed the freedom to grow and to develop. What she meant by that was they needed the freedom of education; they needed freedom to read those documents that they felt were important to them; they needed to be able to engage in conversation, not only with men, but also with other women; she also emphasized the importance of friendship.

Fuller claimed that marriage, at this time in history, needed radical reform to make it more like what she called, "a meeting of the souls." As it stood at this time in the 19th century, marriage was based on what she called, "convenience and utility" designed solely that a woman could find a protector and could also establish a home.

A number of these ideas harkened back to earlier English feminists. I am thinking of a figure such as Mary Wollstonecraft, but in the case of Margaret Fuller, they have a particularly American stamp. What I mean by that is that Fuller emphasizes the notion of female liberty, and she ties female liberty to the idea of a democracy that would apply to all individuals. Here is the quotation that perhaps sums up this view most clearly, quoting from Fuller's *Woman in the Nineteenth Century*, first published in this form in 1845:

> By Man I mean both man and woman; these are the two halves of one thought. I lay no especial stress on the welfare of either. I believe that the development of one cannot be effected without that of the other. My highest wish is that this truth should be distinctly and rationally apprehended, and the condition of life and freedom recognized as the same for the daughters and the sons of time; twin exponents of a divine thought

Fuller was powerfully influenced by Emerson and other Transcendentalists, but soon in her adult life, she found herself influencing these men's thinking as well as the thinking of many individuals. Emerson had actually invited her to join meetings of the Transcendentalist circle as early as 1838, during the second year of its existence. Within a year of that time, when it was needed to decide who would be the first editor of *The Dial* journal, Fuller was actually chosen by Emerson for that very important position. She soon found herself writing large sections of the journal in her own words at the same time that she was corresponding with, and editing the works of, Emerson himself, of Thoreau, of Alcott, of Channing and of many others.

Here is a quote from Emerson that suggests how important she seemed at the time, "She was an active, inspiring companion and correspondent, and all the art, the thought, the nobleness in New England seemed at that moment related to her and she to it."

By "that moment" here, Emerson is referring to that influential decade of the 1830s. In fact, Emerson's lecture entitled "Woman," which he delivered to the Women's Rights Convention that was held in Boston in 1855, is a direct result of Fuller's influence on him.

She was indeed sufficiently forward looking and also frank enough to link the topic of human sexuality and the issue of gender to women's rights, but also significantly, to men's rights. She argued for what now sounds like a very modern need, to re-imagine what we would call gender roles. She claimed that "there is no wholly masculine man," but she also added that there was "no purely feminine woman." She is clearly trying to break down gender boundaries in all sorts of ways.

She was influenced by the Polish Romantic writer, Adam Mickiewicz, the poet of Romantic, if sometimes illicit, love. She met and admired George Sand, the cross-dressing female novelist in France, notorious for her combination of social activism and sexual promiscuity. In fact, Fuller was, to some people, by the time she went to Europe, also a version of a scandalous scarlet woman, whose own ideas about sexual freedom led to an illegitimate child of Fuller's and also a marriage to her Italian lover, the Marquis d'Ossoli, who was then 10 years younger than she. This so-called "natural marriage" was also described as a *Fourierist* marriage. Fourier was a socialist thinker of the time, who argued that as long as two people felt that they were sufficiently in love, they could declare their own marriage—but of course, unmarried lovers, an illegitimate child; we can imagine how the public responded to Fuller by this time.

Indeed she alienated some people because of a personality that was variously described in a series of rather non-complimentary terms. She was called strident, energetic and intense; even those last two words, energetic and intense, were words that would have created problems as a description of women at this point. Nathaniel Hawthorne and James Russell Lowell, both ended up caricaturing Fuller in print, while Sophia Peabody, who married Nathaniel Hawthorne, actually referred to Fuller as "Queen Margaret," not in a positive sense.

It is the case that Fuller's life consistently embodied her skills and her ideals, whatever other people thought of her attitudes and her actions. She had been extremely precocious as a child, as I have noted, learning Latin and many other subjects from a very demanding father who, while he was alive, clearly set a standard that I think she worked to follow throughout her adult life.

She began her professional career as a school teacher at Bronson Alcott's famous Temple School and then at the Green Street School in Providence, Rhode Island. After two years, quite uncharacteristically for women at this time, she resigned her teaching post. The reason that she did so was that she claimed that she needed more time in order to pursue her own writing career, again, something surprising for a woman to say.

Her most original and influential professional activity outside of her written work was a series of organized conversations that she held for groups of women. From 1839 to 1844, she held her series of these so-called "Conversations" in Boson. It was a very simple plan; she encouraged women to gather together, to think and to talk about their own ideas and about the ideas of others. I think it is hard for us now to appreciate the radical nature of this idea, but in Fuller's own time, an intellectual circle of women, free to express their own thoughts, was looked on a really remarkable activity.

It is also the case that she was following, in these conversations, in the footsteps of Elizabeth Palmer Peabody, who had held earlier "reading parties" for women. This notion of conversation of this formal intellectual kind was also influenced by Bronson Alcott's idea for co-educational conversations, in which men and women would gather together to discuss more than simply small talk.

Fuller's friend, Sophia Dana Ripley, who was the wife of George Ripley and one of the Founders with Alcott of the Brook Farm community, helped Fuller to gather together these women for conversations around a series of topics. An example would be, "What were we born to do? How shall we do it?" This gives a suggestion of how broad and significant these conversations might be. The actual meeting place for these conversations was almost always the parlor of Elizabeth Palmer Peabody's home, about which we will learn more in a subsequent lecture.

About two dozen women appeared for the first of these meetings and many other women soon found what they described as a "new and surprising intellectual outlet" in this context. It was also true that these dialogs led Fuller directly to her most significant work, that was the book entitled *Woman in the Nineteenth Century*. She had published an essay called "The Great Lawsuit: Man Versus Men. Woman Versus Women" in *The Dial* in July 1843. This was shortly after Emerson had replaced her as editor. She edited *The Dial* for a period of two years and then Emerson took over for the last two years of that journal's existence. This journalistic essay was then revised and appeared in 1845 as the complete work, *Woman in the Nineteenth Century*. This was a volume that argued quite simply for the end of women's subordination in every sense of that term and for a new view of women's lives as free individuals who had rights to determine important aspects of their own lives.

Her logic in the book is clear and concise. I will do my best to summarize it briefly. She notes, significantly I think, that even liberal men, that is to say even men who might have given lip service to the idea of rights for women, were often hypocrites because these liberal, often Transcendentalist men were advocating complete racial freedom in terms of the abolition of slavery, while they still wanted to restrict women's rights in a whole series of ways, most often centered around domesticity. Likewise, she argued that these same men could claim that women were physically and emotionally unable to assume responsible positions in society, but that women were appropriate for rigorous farm work in the outdoors, as well as probably the most demanding and important task in any society, the raising and the education of young children. One of the things that Fuller wanted to do consistently was to point out these contradictions in even the minds of well meaning men.

She linked what was then called "the woman question"—what were the rights of women and how were they going to be brought about?—which was then being hotly debated not only in America, but also in England. She linked this "woman question" directly to the Emersonian idea of self-reliance. She wrote, "What woman needs is not as a woman to act or rule, but as a nature to grow, as an intellect to discern, as a soul to live freely and unimpeded, to unfold such powers as were given her when we left our common home."

Here we see that simple appeal to natural law, the idea that all people, regardless of whether they happen to be male or female, have certain rights in common, and the simple fact that every woman simply needs to be able to unfold her capacities, not necessarily to act or to rule anyone. It is also worth noting that Fuller in no way ignored men. In fact, she praised a whole series of earlier writers, especially English Romantic writers such as Percy Shelley, Wordsworth and Byron. She praised them for their understanding of women, but especially for their sympathetic depictions of women characters and women's situation throughout their own writings.

In 1843, she traveled on an extensive tour of the Great Lakes with her good friend, Sarah Freeman Clarke, and produced another very widely distributed work called *Summer on the Lakes*. The book was so well written, and it presented such an insightful, almost sociological analysis, as well as a beautiful geographic depiction of the American Midwest, that this was the point at which the newspaper editor, Horace Greeley, invited her to begin work, first as a book reviewer and a review editor for his *New York Tribune*. She flourished almost immediately in this job, and she soon moved, very surprisingly for this era, into a wider role as a general commentator on art and the wider culture.

By 1846, Greeley invited her to become a foreign correspondent, an almost unheard of position. She was one of the first journalists in America to be asked to serve in this capacity, and certainly one of the first women. She traveled almost immediately to Europe, and once there, quickly met and befriended a remarkable group of individuals, including people such as Thomas Carlyle—who we have already seen was so important to Emerson—George Sand and many artists, intellectuals and politicians. It is clear that the experience in Europe opened up a whole new range of ideas and experiences that she would have never had, had she stayed in America.

She actually arrived in Italy in 1847, where she met and fell almost immediately in love with the Marquis Giovanni Angelo d'Ossoli and within a year, gave birth to an illegitimate son. Her biographers differ on whether the two ever married officially or not, but it is clear that her relationship with d'Ossoli caused a lot of negative comment from people, especially back in America.

During the siege of Rome by French Troops in 1849, Fuller showed a very practical side by taking on a role as one of the leaders of a Roman hospital during this time of military conflict. At this point, her husband was fighting actively as an Italian partisan and Fuller found herself very caught up in these energetic political and military events of the time.

As a result, she also met Giuseppe Mazzini, the famous Italian patriot whose strong brand of 19th-century socialism clearly resonated with Fuller's own ideas about women's rights and about human rights more generally. When the Italian cause collapsed rather suddenly, she decided to return to America, a step—as I have noted—that turned out to have tragic consequences.

She became as famous in death as in life, however, partly because of the circumstances of her drowning at age 40. She had sailed from Europe to America with d'Ossoli and their son in May 1850. The ship's captain died on the journey and an inexperienced sailor apparently took over the vessel. Then the ship went down in a terrible storm, but while actually in sight of Fire Island. As those of you who know Long Island will know, almost at the mouth of the New York Harbor.

Emerson, as I said, sent Thoreau to recover her manuscripts, which they knew to have been with her, from the wreckage. But Thoreau wrote a powerful letter in which he described the desolate beach—within days of the shipwreck—with only unidentifiable human remains and a few broken ship's timbers.

Nevertheless, and even given this tragic ending at such a young age, Fuller's influence has been extensive, but in interesting ways, it has also been variable over time. I will try to explain what I mean by that. By 1881, about three decades after her death, the suffragettes, Susan B. Anthony and Elizabeth Cady Stanton, could claim—this is a quote from one of their works—they said that Fuller "possessed more influence on the thought of American women than any woman previous to her time." That is fairly high praise from two of the most influential suffragettes of the 19th century—that no woman in America has had more influence on the way women thought than Margaret Fuller.

She contributed significantly to that movement that we have come to call the American Renaissance in literature. In addition to her writings, as I have tried to suggest, she was also widely known in her own time for her engagement with various 19th-century reform movements. Once again, we see that interesting Transcendentalist combination between the more abstract intellectual and the very practical applied social thinker. She was described as brilliant by almost everyone who met her, and this clearly accounted for some of the power of her influence. It is without doubt that she intellectually challenged the likes of Emerson and numerous other male thinkers, who ordinarily would have been seen as the only gender available to that kind of ascendancy at the time.

The women who attended her Conversations, which we have discussed, and many men of the time who came to know her, actually described her influence on them as life altering. I think if we needed an analogy, today we would say that being in her Conversation groups, or even knowing her, could be associated with modern consciousness raising or a kind of self-help session, where people would encounter Fuller and would come away either knowing something about their own rights in the case of women, or knowing something about themselves in the case of almost everyone who met her.

It should be obvious by now that her major work, *Woman in the Nineteenth Century*, had a direct influence on the women's rights movement. Here again is a simple quote that sums up the message of that work, I think. Fuller said, "Women need, especially at this juncture, a much greater range of occupation than they have, to rouse their latent powers." That very simple sense of powers that are latent—with the implication that those powers are being wasted—and that women, especially at this moment in history, simply need a range of opportunities that will allow those capacities to flourish.

The book is now considered a classic, not only of American literature, but also of, more specifically, feminist thinking. Its influence was powerfully experienced as early as a gathering of women's rights advocates, the first major gathering of this kind, at Seneca Falls, New York, only three years after the work was published. In this case, the timing was significant.

By putting her own principles into action in her own life in what were seen as extreme ways, it is also the case that she sometimes alienated other people. It is obvious that any of the claims she was making about the rights of women at the time, could have been seen as controversial to more conservative males and, as we have seen, to females of the time. But when we consider the details of her own life, we also see that it was her actions as well that might have distanced her from many of the people that surrounded her. In this sense, her influence was affected by a number of people who sought to criticize her, as well as a number who, over time, worked almost to protect her reputation.

The great American novelist, Nathaniel Hawthorne, described her as what he called "a great humbug." He has a character named Zenobia in his novel, *The Blithedale Romance*, which was the satirical novel about the Brook Farm Transcendentalist community. This character was based largely on Fuller; his "great humbug." On the other side of the equation, there were later editors such as William Henry Channing, another member of that important Channing family, and James Freeman Clarke, who worked, in a sense, to soften the intensity of some of Fuller's ideas. The two of them published a collection in 1852 called *Memoirs of Margaret Fuller Ossoli*, and they actually ended up rewriting passages from her correspondence and striking out what they saw as offensive passages from her journal. In this case it was male authors trying to protect her reputation, who expurgated and altered part of her writing in order to, I suppose we would say, make her more palatable to a wider audience.

By the 1960s, in any case, the modern women's movement had revived intense interest in Fuller's life and work. If one goes to the scholarly resources now, one will find a great deal of scholarship that has appeared about Fuller, especially since the late-1960s. It certainly is the case that she is now taught in many college and university classes throughout the country and there is an active scholarly society that is dedicated to the study of her work and her influence.

Now, from this extremely significant single female individual, we will turn to a group of women, all of whom had important roles in the Transcendentalist movement.

Lecture Fourteen
Transcendental Women

Scope:

Transcendentalist thinking was not only a family affair, but it was also a women's movement, at least in the minds of many of its practitioners. Men in the movement supported women, worked side by side with them, and argued for their rights. Women, just as importantly, seized the mantle of their own authority and argued strongly for their own causes: religious freedom, the abolition of slavery, and women's personal rights to own property, cast votes, and control their destinies. This lecture will explore a group of women who had a direct and powerful impact on Transcendentalist ways of thinking, from the three remarkable Peabody sisters to less well-known women, including the radical abolitionist Lydia Child and the indefatigable Caroline Dall. Even more famous social crusaders, such as Elizabeth Cady Stanton and Lucretia Mott, although not directly connected to members of the Transcendentalist circle, deserve mention among the women who were inspired by or helped to inspire American Transcendentalism.

Outline

I. Women were central to the Transcendentalist movement from its earliest beginnings.

    A. Many of the leading New England families produced women of note.

        1. Emerson's family had several important women: Mary Moody Emerson, his intellectual and Puritanical aunt; his wife, Lidian (formerly Lydia); and his daughter, who inspired Alcott to write her first book.

        2. The Alcott family produced not only Louisa May but also May, who was a well-known artist, and two other sisters who figured in *Little Women*.

        3. Reverend Channing's daughter attended the Peabody sisters' school and helped to bring Channing and Elizabeth Peabody together.

        4. Margaret Fuller's volume *Woman in the Nineteenth Century* (1845), as we have seen, emphasized the role of women throughout history and called on women to seize their legitimate power.

   B. Transcendentalism emphasized the value of women to their families and society.

   1. Education had been the province of women as mothers, sisters, and teachers.

   2. Many women were drawn to activism by social causes: abolition, the right to vote, nursing and health, poverty and inequality.

   3. The inherent equality of people logically had to include half the human race.

   4. Women's traditional roles as wives and mothers were seen as hindering but also advancing their cause.

II. The Peabody parents, a doctor and a teacher, produced a powerful group of daughters.

   A. Elizabeth Peabody (1804–1894) was the eldest and attended a school run by her mother that encouraged girls in literate skills and the fulfillment of their potential.

   1. Emerson was Elizabeth's private Greek tutor. She went on to establish her own school and to serve as a teacher in Bronson Alcott's Temple School and as an amanuensis for Dr. William Ellery Channing, her preacher.

   2. By 1839, Elizabeth published Jones Very's *Poems and Essays* and, thus, became one of the first woman publishers in America. In the coming years, she would publish, in order, Dr. Channing's *Emancipation* (1840), Nathaniel Hawthorne's *Liberty Tree* (1841), two volumes of *The Dial* (1842–1843), and *Aesthetic Papers* (1849), in which Thoreau's "Resistance to Civil Government" appeared for the first time.

   3. In 1840 Elizabeth opened the West Street Bookstore at the front of her house, which became a central gathering place for Transcendentalists for more than a decade. Margaret Fuller's "Conversations" for women began here, and the Brook Farm commune was planned here.

   4. By 1859, Elizabeth adapted the ideas of Friedrich Froebel, a German educator, into the beginnings of the kindergarten movement in America. She rejected discipline based on fear, as Alcott had done, but she argued, against Alcott, that too much introspection was a bad thing for children.

5. Together, Elizabeth and her sister Mary wrote *Moral Culture of Infancy and Kindergarten Guide* (1863) and supported the idea of public kindergarten, especially in impoverished neighborhoods.

6. Theodore Parker, the activist abolitionist minister, praised Elizabeth as "a woman of most astonishing powers [...] rare qualities of head and heart [...] A good analyst of character, a free spirit, kind, generous, noble." The novelist Henry James, on the other hand, caricatured her as the absent-minded and somewhat nosey Miss Birdseye in *The Bostonians*.

7. By the end of her long life, Elizabeth had also been an advocate for rights for Native Americans and the vote for women, had supported political refugees from overseas, and had fought for world peace. All this activity was pervaded by a Transcendentalist sense that a spiritual unity of God, man, and nature might transform individuals and the wider society.

B. Her sister Mary (1807–1887), like Elizabeth, was an influential schoolteacher and one of the founders of the kindergarten movement in America.

1. In early life, the two sisters began a girl's school in Brookline.

2. Mary later married the educational reformer Horace Mann and went on, with Elizabeth, to import educational ideas for the very young.

3. Mary wrote *Christianity in the Kitchen* (1858), which argued that healthy nutrition had a moral basis. The cookbook also contributed to the later fame of the Boston School of Cooking.

4. Mary went on to be coauthor of Elizabeth's major work on the kindergarten movement and to advocate for a sensitive approach to early education.

5. Throughout adult life, she supported her husband's career as a public school advocate, a reformist congressman, and later, president of Antioch College.

C. The third sister, Sophia (1809–1871), is best known as the wife of Nathaniel Hawthorne.

   1. Sophia had watched Nathaniel as a boy in their Salem neighborhood.

   2. After their marriage, they lived in the Old Manse until forced out because they could not pay the rent. Hawthorne's career did not take off until the success of *The Scarlet Letter* (1850).

   3. Hawthorne often depicted her as frail, sickly, and ethereal, his "angel-in-the-house," his "Dove," but recent scholarship sees these descriptions as inaccurate.

   4. In fact, Sophia was a successful painter and illustrator and a well-traveled woman before her marriage. Later, she was a supporter of Hawthorne's career as a writer and diplomat, as well as mother to his three children.

   5. Her insights and Transcendental ethos are clearly evident in a quote from her journal; describing a morning in the forest, she recalled: "I held my breath to hear the breathing of the spirit around me […] Man has a universe within him as well as without." Two decades later, Thoreau would say the same.

III. Numerous other women warrant emphasis because they influenced or were influenced by the Transcendentalist circle, even when they were not directly linked to its members or activities.

   A. Lydia Maria Child (1802–1880) was another remarkably active woman.

   1. From her birth in Wayland, Massachusetts, she went on to have an influence as an outspoken and influential abolitionist, a women's rights advocate, a supporter of Native American rights, a novelist, and journalist.

   2. Child is best remembered for "Over the River and Through the Woods."

   3. Her 1833 book, *An Appeal in Favor of That Class of Americans Called Africans*, was a very early work by a white person in support of abolition.

   4. Child noted that slavery went directly against Christian doctrine and degraded not only slaves but slave owners, as well. She did not exempt the North from her criticisms: "I am fully aware of the unpopularity of the task I have undertaken," she wrote in the introduction, "but though I expect ridicule and censure, it is not in my nature to fear them."

B. Caroline Dall (1822–1912) was a child prodigy who attended a series of Emerson's lectures at the age of 12.

    1. Her father, responding to those who said that he was wasting a ticket, said, "I shall expect her to write abstracts of them."

    2. Her most important publication was the sweeping volume, *The College, the Market, and the Court; Or, Woman's Relation to Education, Labor, and Law* (1867); as a long-time activist in the American Social Science Association, she advocated for improved prison conditions, treatments for the insane, and public health.

    3. Dall's journal, which she compiled for almost 75 years, has been called one of the most complete records of a woman's life in the 19th century.

C. Numerous suffragettes, along with other important women of the era, while not always a direct part of Transcendentalist circles, drew ideas and inspiration from the movement.

    1. Elizabeth Cady Stanton (1815–1902) organized the first women's rights convention in the United States in Seneca Falls, New York (1848). Out of this meeting came resolutions demanding rights for women, including better educational and employment opportunities and the right to vote.

    2. Lucretia Mott (1793–1880) attended the World Anti-Slavery Convention in 1840 in London, where she met Elizabeth Cady Stanton. The men in charge of this convention refused to seat her and the other women delegates. Partly as a result of this treatment, she became a co-organizer of the Seneca Falls Convention.

    3. Julia Ward Howe (1819–1910) wrote the *Battle Hymn of the Republic* after a visit to a Union Army camp on the banks of the Potomac River near Washington, D.C., in 1861. There, she heard the song "John Brown's Body" sung by soldiers, and in her own words, she acted on an idea of direct inspiration that goes back to the Romantics: "I sprang out of bed and in the dimness found an old stump of a pen, which I remembered using the day before. I scrawled the verses almost without looking at the paper."

4. "His truth is marching on," is a quintessentially Transcendentalist idea. A divine spirituality is embodied in a religious and social action designed to "make men free" but also to make women free.

Essential Reading:

Marshall, Megan. *The Peabody Sisters: Three Women Who Ignited American Romanticism.*

Baym, Nina. "The Ann Sisters: Elizabeth Peabody's Millennial Historicism."

Supplementary Reading:

Deese, Helen R. "Emerson from a Feminist Perspective: The Caroline H. Dall Journals."

Karcher, Caroline L. *The First Woman in the Republic: A Cultural Biography of Lydia Maria Child.*

Questions to Consider:

1. How did both men and women contribute to the important roles played by women in the 19th century?

2. What connections, if any, can be drawn between the role of women in American Transcendentalism and the feminist movement from the 1960s to the present?

Lecture Fourteen—Transcript
Transcendental Women

From a single remarkable woman in Margaret Fuller, we now turn to a remarkable group of Transcendentalist women. Transcendentalist thinking was not only a family affair; it was also a women's movement, at least in the minds of many of its practitioners. Almost all of the men in the Movement supported women in various ways, worked side by side with them and often argued for their increasing rights. Just as important, women seized the mantle of their own growing authority and argued strongly for their own causes: religious freedom, that abolition of slavery, and perhaps most of all, women's personal rights to own property, cast votes and control their destinies in any number of ways.

This lecture will explore a group of women who had a direct and a powerful impact on a range of Transcendentalist ideas—from the three remarkable Peabody sisters to less well known women, such as the radical abolitionist, Lydia Child and the indefatigable Caroline Dall. Even more famous social crusaders of the time, such as Elizabeth Cady Stanton and Lucretia Mott, although not necessarily directly connected to members of the Transcendentalist circle, will deserve a mention in this lecture, among those women who were inspired by, or who helped to inspire, the wider movement known as American Transcendentalism.

Women were clearly central to the Transcendentalist movement from its earliest beginnings. Many of the leading New England families that we have discussed produced significant women of note. Ralph Waldo Emerson's family had a number of important women. I in addition to his mother, whom we have already mentioned; his intellectual and puritanical aunt, Mary Moody Emerson; his wife, Lydian, and even his young daughter, who, as we noted in our last lecture, inspired Louisa May Alcott to write her first book. That famous Alcott family produced not only Louisa May, but also her sister, May, who became a well known artist, as well as the two other sisters who figured so prominently in *Little Women*.

Reverend William Ellery Channing's daughter attended the Peabody sisters' school and helped to bring Channing and Elizabeth Peabody together, a linkage that we will discuss in some detail. And as we have just seen, Margaret Fuller's volume, *Woman in the Nineteenth*

Century, first published in book form in 1845, emphasized not only the role of women throughout history, but also made an important call on women to seize their legitimate powers and also their legitimate political rights.

Transcendentalism, as a Movement, emphasized the value of women not only to society, but also to their families. Education throughout history had often been the province of women, first as mothers, but in many cases, as sisters and even outside of the familial context, as teachers. The important connection between Transcendentalist ways of thinking and educational ideas almost necessarily would have to include women in those discussions.

A number of women, at this time, were drawn to forms of activism by the social causes that were the mainstays of discussion in men's circles and increasingly among women. I am thinking of the Abolitionist Movement, the question of the right to vote, issues about nursing and public health and also the complicated relationship between poverty and inequality, as we will see.

Of course, as proponents of women's rights had argued already in Europe, the inherent equality of human beings logically had to include half of the human race. If, since the 18th century, and certainly in the founding documents of our own country, we were arguing for the inherent rights of all human beings, we would have to include 50 percent of humanity in those discussions. It is also the case, if we think about the conversations on the issue of women's rights at the time, that women's traditional roles, primarily as wives and mothers, were seen as hindering their cause in some way, but also advancing their cause in other ways. First in terms of the relationship between mothers and the powerful influence they have over their own children, but also increasingly among Transcendentalists in terms of the roles that wives might play in their husbands' developing ideas and also the role that men and women could play in more shared intellectual, and eventually social, activity.

Let us begin with the Peabody family. The Peabody parents—the father was a doctor and the mother was a teacher—produced a group of three remarkable daughters, each significant in her own way. First is Elizabeth Peabody, who was the eldest of the sisters and who attended, first, a school run by her own mother that encouraged girls not only in the literate skills, which had often been the province of women, but also in the wider fulfillment of their potential. Elizabeth Peabody was quite lucky as a young girl; Ralph Waldo Emerson was her private Greek tutor. As a result of the wide-ranging education she received from her mother and the likes of Emerson, she went on to establish, first, her own school, and then to serve as a teacher in that school of Bronson Alcott's, the Temple School. Additionally, as an amanuensis—that is a 19th-century term for a copyist, someone who copies the writings of another person—for Dr. William Ellery Channing, another of our lecture subjects, who was actually her own preacher in the church she attended.

By 1839, she turned in a slightly different direction, especially for a woman, and she published *Poems and Essays* by a poet named Jones Very, whom we will discuss in a later lecture, and at this point became one of the first female publishers in America. In the coming years, Elizabeth Peabody would go on to publish the following works in chronological order: Dr. Channing's work entitled *Emancipation*, an early-1840 work on that subject; Nathaniel Hawthorne's *Liberty Tree*, published in 1841; two volumes of the journal, *The Dial*, both 1842 and 1843, were published by Peabody; and finally, *Aesthetic Papers* in 1849, a volume whose title we have already heard because it was the book in which Thoreau's essay entitled, "Resistance to Civil Government" appeared for the first time. Clearly, by 1850, Elizabeth Peabody was one of the most significant publishers in New England and certainly one of the only women publishers.

In 1840, Elizabeth had opened the West Street Bookstore at the front of her own house. This famous bookshop became a gathering place for Transcendentalists for over a decade. Margaret Fuller's "Conversations" for women, about which we heard a great deal in our previous lecture, actually began in this same parlor bookshop and the Brook Farm utopian community was planned here. Thus, Elizabeth Peabody was seen at the center of a series of intellectual and social activities that brought together a lot of the individuals we have been talking about.

By 1859, in yet another expansion of her ideas, Elizabeth had adopted the ideas of Friedrich Froebel, a German educator, who had advocated education for the very young and it was Elizabeth's appropriation of Froebel's ideas that many have seen as the start of the Kindergarten Movement in America; yet another connection between Transcendentalist thinking and American education. She rejected any educational notion of discipline of the young based on fear. As we saw earlier, the general principle in the 19th century was that you instilled fear in children that would force them to learn the information you were dispensing. Peabody, like Alcott before her, rejected the idea that you could ever build a meaningful form of discipline on the idea of fear. But she separated herself from Alcott and claimed that introspection, too much focus on thinking about the self, could actually be a bad thing for children. I point that out simply by way of saying that Elizabeth Peabody had her own ideas in addition to the other influences that came into her thinking.

Together, Elizabeth and her sister, Mary, wrote a very important volume called *Moral Culture of Infancy and Kindergarten Guide*; it was published in 1863 and it supported, for the first time in the United States, the idea of public kindergarten, of the value of the this form of education for very young children. But they went beyond advocating simply the idea of kindergarten to arguing that it was especially important in impoverished neighborhoods where children were not receiving certain forms of education from their parents and would therefore, benefit from this public form of education at an early age.

Theodore Parker, that activist abolitionist minister, praised Elizabeth in high terms. Here is what he said, "She was a woman of most astonishing powers...rare qualities of head and heart...a good analyst of character, a free spirit, kind, generous, noble."

Once again, very high praise from one of the powerful men of the period, about how many aspects of Elizabeth's personality could be of value to others. At the same time, and on the other hand, the novelist, Henry James, caricatured her as the absent-minded and somewhat nosy Ms. Birdseye in his famous novel, *The Bostonians*.

By the end of Elizabeth's long life, she had been an advocate for rights not only of women, but also for Native Americans. She had supported political refugees from overseas, which became an increasingly important topic as the century proceeded, and she actually argued for a version of world peace which would have seemed much more appropriate in the middle of the 20th century than 100 years earlier.

All of her activity was pervaded by what we would have to see now as a Transcendentalist sense, that there was a possibility for the spiritual unity between God, men and women and nature, that had the capacity not only to transform the individuals who felt this unity, but also could have a much stronger impact on the society at large.

Now we will turn to Elizabeth's sister, Mary. Her sister, like Elizabeth, was an influential school teacher and, as I have suggested, one of the founders of the Kindergarten Movement in America. I think we tend to take institutions such as kindergarten almost for granted in our own time. I think it is interesting to think back on a time in history when this idea was almost unheard of and to see how closely some of those Transcendentalist principles, including even the philosophical and theological underpinnings, might link to the idea that it is a good idea to have children in school as early as possible.

In their early life, these two sisters, Elizabeth and Mary, had actually begun a girls' school in Brookline, Massachusetts. Mary would later go on to marry Horace Mann, another educational reformer of the period. With Elizabeth's influence, she and Mann were both partly responsible for bringing these educational ideas to the very young. Mary also wrote an interesting work called *Christianity in the Kitchen*, which argued—again, well ahead of her time—that healthy nutrition was not only good for the body, but that it might also have a moral basis, that people who ate a certain diet might be likely to actually become better people. The cookbook was not incidental, but it ended up contributing to the later fame of the Boston School of Cooking, which became one of the most successful cooking schools in America.

As we have seen, Mary became the co-author of Elizabeth's major work on the importance of the establishment of kindergartens and more generally—and I think the really important point for us now—is the idea of the importance of a sensitive approach to early education. For a long period in human history, children were simply seen as small adults and there was a sense in which adults simply waited for children to grow up in order to start treating them as adults treated one another. I think if we follow the movements in educational theory through the 19th century, even through our Transcendentalist figures, we will see how there is an increasing appreciation of the significance of experience to even the very young. These are obviously ideas that even anticipate the thinking of someone such as Freud, who clearly argues that the experiences we have even before we are five or six years old can be extremely influential in developing our adult personality.

Throughout Mary Peabody's adult life, she supported her husband's career, first as a public school advocate, later as a reformist congressman and finally as president of Antioch College. Here was a woman who was able to be a close companion of her husband not only in the traditional sense of that term, but also in her ability to support his career while advancing her own.

The third Peabody sister, Sophia, is now best known probably as the wife of the author, Nathaniel Hawthorne. They had all grown up in the same neighborhood and Sophia reported later in life that she had actually watched him first as a very young boy in their Salem, Massachusetts neighborhood, the same Salem famous for the witchcraft trials.

After Sophia's marriage to Nathaniel Hawthorne, they lived in that famous house, the Old Manse, which had also been a home of Emerson until they were forced out because they were unable to pay the rent. We think of a writer such as Nathaniel Hawthorne now and we have a hard time imagining a point in his life when he would not have been able to keep up with the rent. But like so many literary figures, Hawthorne's career did not really take off until the success of *The Scarlet Letter*, the work for which he is probably still best known, and that was not until 1850. Therefore, his early adult life was under much more strained circumstances.

Hawthorne, himself, often depicted Sophia as rather frail, as sickly and certainly as ethereal. He called her his "Dove" and this image of her fit in very well with what, at the time, would have been considered the angel-in-the-house ideal, the notion that a woman was simply a kind of almost ghostly figure who would travel through the domestic sphere, making sure that especially the men's lives were managed in an appropriate way. And Hawthorne, in many of his descriptions of Sophia, fit her into that characteristic.

It is now clear that recent scholarships show that most of those descriptions were largely inaccurate or at least they were exaggerations. In fact, Sophia was a successful painter and illustrator throughout her adult life and she had been an extremely well traveled woman, even before she married Hawthorne. Later on, she became a supporter again of Hawthorne's career as a writer and subsequently as a diplomat, and of course, she was the mother of his three children—once again, that aspect of women's lives that is often passed over in discussions about their vigorousness and their strength. To rear those three children was no small accomplishment.

Sophia's insights and even her transcendental ethos are evident in a quotation from her own journal. Once again, we see all of these women keeping journals under the influence of the idea that that processing of your own thought patterns in writing is advantageous to your self-development. Here she is, in that journal, describing a morning in the forest, "I held my breath to hear the breathing of the spirit around me...Man has a universe within him as well as without." I quote that passage simply to remind us that two decades later Thoreau would say almost exactly the same thing, sitting at the doorway of his cabin by Walden Pond.

Now I would like to turn to numerous other women who warrant emphasis in this lecture because they influenced the Transcendentalist circle or because they were influenced by its members. I am thinking here, as I have suggested, about a group of women who include some who were not directly linked to the circle or its members, but who clearly had influences that may have gone in both directions.

First, let us consider Lydia Maria Child, another remarkably active woman who lived for almost eight decades at a time when that was a remarkably long life. From her birth in Wayland, Massachusetts, she went on in her adult life, to have influence as an extremely outspoken and also influential abolitionist. She supported women's rights; she supported Indian rights at a time when that was also not seen in quite the same terms as other human rights issues; and she was also an influential novelist and journalist.

Nowadays, like a number of figures that history sometimes tends to pass over, she is probably best remembered for a lyric she penned on one occasion, "Over the River and Through the Woods," that famous little poem that we all say among our families at Thanksgiving. Here again is a remarkable female figure who, in terms of her historical influence, has been distilled down to a very small bit of memory, but whose actual activities extended much more widely.

She wrote a book in 1833, whose title was *An Appeal in Favor of That Class of Americans Called Africans*—1833 remember—this was a very early work by a white person in support of the absolute abolition of slavery, three decades before the Civil War. I also would like you to consider that title in detail, *An Appeal in Favor of That Class of Americans Called Africans*. Even the syntax of that title suggests that the first reference she wants to apply to these people is as Americans and she also wants to suggest that she has to present an appeal in order to support what obviously becomes a defense of the rights of the people we now see as African-Americans.

Child noted in this early work, that slavery went directly against all Christian doctrine and she also made the quite sophisticated argument for the time that suggested that slavery degraded not only slaves, but slave owners as well. Here is what she said about her work, since she knew that she would not be exempt from criticism, she wrote in her introduction, "I am fully aware of the unpopularity of the task I have undertaken, but though I expect ridicule and censure, it is not in my nature to fear them."

It is also worth noting that Child actually claimed that the North should not be exempt from criticisms from slavery either, remember that slavery had existed in the North almost as long as it would in the South.

Another important female figure is Caroline Dall, a child prodigy who attended a series of Emerson's lectures when she was still only 12 years old. Her father responded to a number of people who said that he might be wasting a ticket by giving it to his 12-year-old daughter; he said, "I shall expect her to write abstracts of them," that is to say, of Emerson's lectures. Here once again, we see the powerful influence that a strong-willed father or mother could have, especially on the education of a young child.

Dall's most important publication was a wide-ranging volume; consider the title—*The College, the Market, and the Court; Or, Woman's Relation to Education, Labor, and Law*. This work was published in 1867 and, as it suggests, she advocated for a whole range of improved aspects of women's lives—their education, their ability to work and their interaction with the legal system. She was a long-time activist in what became the American Social Science Association and she also advocated for improved conditions in prisons, improved treatment of the insane and, for a wide range of public health reforms. She kept a journal for almost 75 years and one historian has called it one of the most complete records of a woman's life in the 19th century.

Numerous suffragettes, along with other important women of this era, while not always directly associated with Transcendentalist circles, drew ideas and inspiration from the movement. Elizabeth Cady Stanton organized the first Women's Rights Convention in the United States, as we have already said, at Seneca Falls, New York in 1848. Out of this meeting came a series of resolutions demanding rights for women, including better educational and employment opportunities as well as the right to vote.

Another important figure, Lucretia Mott, attended the World Anti-Slavery Convention in 1840 in London, where she met this same suffragette, Stanton, for the first time. The men in charge of this anti-slavery convention refused to seat Mott and any other women delegates. Partly as a result of this treatment, she became a co-organizer of the Seneca Falls convention.

Finally, Julia Ward Howe, another name well known to almost all Americans, wrote the *Battle Hymn of the Republic* after a visit to a Union Army Camp on the banks of the Potomac River, not far from Washington, D.C. in 1861. The way that song came about is an interesting story. She heard the soldiers singing the earlier verses of "John Brown's Body," that abolitionist song, written about John Brown and in her own words, she acted on idea that I like to associate with direct inspiration that goes back at least to the British Romantics. Here is what she said about the authorship of the *Battle Hymn of the Republic*, "I sprang out of bed and in the dimness found an old stump of a pen which I remembered using the day before. I scrawled the verses almost without looking at the paper."

This idea that a person could have an experience, then suddenly a fully formed set of verses would spring into their head—almost without their own rational knowledge—which they would then write down as fast as possible, before they might forget them, is associated with a whole series of Transcendentalist ideas about intuitive knowledge and about our connection to wider truths.

Indeed, the phrase, "His truth is marching on," is a quintessentially Transcendentalist idea. Let us think about it for a moment: "His truth is marching on." A divine spirituality is embodied in a religious and social action, designed to make men free, but also to make women free as well.

With that, we will turn to one of the few Transcendentalists who hailed from the southern states, Moncure Conway.

Lecture Fifteen
Moncure Conway—Southern Transcendentalist

Scope:

Moncure Conway's life unfolded in ways that proved indicative of the history of Transcendentalism. His life also reveals why Transcendentalism was primarily a northern movement. Conway was a Virginian, born to a wealthy family near Fredericksburg, a town that took on crucial significance during the Civil War. He attended Dickinson College in Pennsylvania, where he read Emerson for the first time. While studying at Harvard Divinity School, he met Emerson, Thoreau, and Alcott. He became an avid abolitionist under the influence of Theodore Parker, much to the astonishment of his aristocratic southern family. Conway's own influence grew in England, where he moved to live, preach, and finally, to become famous as a public lecturer. In England, he befriended Carlyle, Dickens, and Darwin, among many other leading lights. He evolved from the idealism of Emerson, through the applied activism of Parker, toward a very modern liberal humanism. Unable to retain the consistent optimism he attributed to Emerson, he eventually abandoned the organized church altogether. To this day, Conway Hall in London's Red Lion Square stands as a memorial to his influence.

Outline

I. Moncure Conway (1832–1907) was one of the few southerners whose life was transformed by his encounter with Transcendentalism. Why was the movement restricted to New England?

  A. Conway was born in 1832 to a wealthy Virginia family in Falmouth, near Fredericksburg, a city that would change hands many times during the Civil War.

  1. His father and brothers were slaveholders and southern sympathizers.

  2. His mother was more liberal in her thinking, as Moncure also became.

  3. Transcendentalism was little known and less of an influence in the southern states at this time, partly

because agriculture so dominated industry and because conservative denominations still dominated liberal ones.

B. Conway attended Dickinson College in Pennsylvania, at that time a Methodist school.

1. He was first exposed to the ideals of Emerson at Dickinson (1847).

2. At this time, the South was suspicious of Transcendentalism and especially of Emerson, because his egalitarian ideas were a direct threat to an aristocratic, slave-holding society. The pastoral myth could never be fully democratic.

3. Conway wrote a youthful letter to Emerson, in which he claimed to be "a Natural Radical—to whose soul Radicalism is as air to a bird," and he lamented his upbringing among conservative southerners.

C. Conway went north to enter Harvard Divinity School and graduated in 1854. He became a circuit-riding Methodist minister after graduation, but his own religious doubts caused him to become a Unitarian within a year.

1. He soon met Emerson and became close friends with the person he described as his "spiritual father."

2. He also met Alcott and Thoreau and became an abolitionist under the influence of Theodore Parker and William Lloyd Garrison, among others.

3. Here is his description of Thoreau, whom he came to know quite well: "Like the pious Yogi, so long motionless whilst gazing on the sun that knotty plants encircled his neck and the cast snake-skin his loins, and the birds built their nests on his shoulders, this poet and naturalist, by equal consecration a part of the field and the forest."

4. Conway became minister of First Unitarian Church in Washington, D.C., but he was soon dismissed for preaching against slavery as immoral.

5. He took his new wife to Virginia, but she scandalized the family when she embraced and then kissed a young female slave.

6. Conway was well enough known by the Civil War to visit the White House in an effort to convince Lincoln to free all slaves. He failed at the time but then led his own family's escaped slaves to freedom in Ohio.

II. Because of his dissatisfaction with life in America during this time, he moved to England after the Civil War had ended.

    A. In London, Conway continued his career as a social activist and public speaker.

        1. He soon came to know a wide range of England's most influential people: Charles Dickens, Thomas Carlyle, and Charles Darwin.

        2. He wrote, after a visit to Down House, that Darwin "expressed satisfaction that I had been able to derive from evolution the hopeful religion set forth in my discourse, but I remember that he did not express agreement with it."

        3. Conway was able to continue his freethinking ideals (abolition, women's suffrage, complete religious freedom or freedom from religion) in the more conducive and accepting climate in England.

        4. He wrote influential biographies of Emerson (in which he discussed his own disagreements with the master), Hawthorne, and Thomas Paine, all of which contributed to the Transcendentalist cult of the individual.

    B. Conway traveled back and forth between England and America, never feeling quite at home in either place.

        1. After the end of the Civil War, he had not felt comfortable in either the South or North. His ideas were simply too liberal and forward-looking.

        2. He ended up in Paris, where he died in 1907.

        3. Like Emerson and Fuller, he thus contributed to the internationalization of Transcendentalist ideas by traveling overseas and publishing works that were widely read throughout Europe: *Testimonies Concerning Slavery* (1864), *The Sacred Anthology: A Book of Ethical Scriptures* (1874), and an autobiography that appeared three years before his death.

III. Conway, like Emerson before him, eventually left organized religion altogether in favor of a secular and scientific version of spirituality.

A. As he wrote after giving up on the idea of a personal God: "Eyes turned from phantom gods have caught glimpses of a divine life in the evolution of nature, and the mystical movement at the heart of man" ("Christianity," 1876).

    1. His abandonment of religion was spurred in part by the death of his young son, named Emerson, as Darwin's disillusionment was also brought about by his 10-year-old daughter's death.

    2. Conway ended up believing that Emerson was overly optimistic and that hard-nosed materialistic rationalism was the only mode of thought that might approach the truth about the universe.

    3. Not many individuals at this time were willing to push the logic of their skepticism as far as Conway, but such freethinking became a model for many 20th-century intellectuals.

B. Conway's influence remained widespread even after he came to be acknowledged as a radical freethinker.

    1. Mark Twain, Walt Whitman, Elizabeth Cady Stanton, and Andrew Carnegie all contributed funds to a Dickinson College building named after him.

    2. Andrew Carnegie, among many notables, attended his memorial service in New York City in 1907.

    3. Conway Hall in Red Lion Square, in London, founded by the South Place Ethical Society, remains a tribute to his memory. Here, such authors as Salman Rushdie help to continue the sorts of "free speech and progressive thought" once advocated by Conway.

Essential Reading:

Conway, Moncure. *Autobiography: Memories and Experiences of Moncure Daniel Conway.*

John d'Entremont. *Southern Emancipator, Moncure Conway: The American Years, 1832–1865.*

Questions to Consider:

1. Why did a thinker like Conway eventually feel forced to give up on religion altogether?

2. What aspects of life in the American South made it less likely that the ideas of Transcendentalism would take hold there?

Lecture Fifteen—Transcript
Moncure Conway—Southern Transcendentalist

Welcome back. Now we will turn to consider Moncure Conway, a person I like to refer to as the Southern Transcendentalist. Moncure Conway's life unfolded in a series of ways that proved extremely indicative of the history of Transcendentalism. For now, at this moment in our lectures, I think he forms a useful way of drawing together a number of the themes, individuals and ideas that we have discussed.

His life also helps us to understand why Transcendentalism was primarily a northern movement, why its ideas and influences did not extend to include individuals in the southern states, or even in the western part of the United States. Conway was, by birth, a Virginian, born into a wealthy family near Fredericksburg, a town that would take on a crucial significance during the entire Civil War in large measure due to its geographical position, about which we will hear more.

He attended Dickinson College in southern Pennsylvania, where he read Emerson for the first time. It was clearly his reading of Emerson that became one of the most signal and significant experiences of his intellectual life. He then went on from Dickinson to study at the Harvard Divinity School, where he—as we might expect—had the opportunity to meet Emerson, Thoreau and Alcott in the circles around Cambridge, Boston and Concord.

He became what we would have to describe as an avid, or perhaps almost rabid, abolitionist largely under the influence of Theodore Parker and certainly much to the astonishment and dismay of his aristocratic Southern family. Conway's own influence clearly began in New England, but then grew in England, where he had moved to live, to preach and finally to become quite famous as a public lecturer. It was in England that he befriended, once again, Thomas Carlyle, that Victorian Sage who proved so important to so many of the Transcendentalists. But Conway also came to know Charles Dickens quite well, and even Charles Darwin, among many other of the leading lights of Victorian English culture, especially in the areas around London.

There is no sense in which Conway's thinking was static, however. He evolved very clearly over the course of his adulthood, from the idealism of Emerson, through what I think we would call the applied activism of someone such as Theodore Parker, toward what we would have to see as a very modern version of liberal humanism. He eventually was unable to retain that consistent, and almost unrelenting, optimism that he attributed to Emerson and, partly as a result of that, he eventually abandoned the organized church altogether. His reasons for leaving the church were in no way identical to Emerson's but this notion, once again, of not being able to find a formal organized denomination in which to locate his own thinking, as we have seen, was not atypical for the time.

To this day, in fact, a building called Conway Hall in London's Red Lion Square, stands as a memorial to his influence. I will talk more about that by way of conclusion. Moncure Conway, as will be evident by now, was one of the few Southerners whose life was transformed by his early encounter with Transcendentalism. As a way of beginning this lecture, I would really like to frame that question for you—why was it that Transcendentalism was restricted to such an extent to New England? Along the way I hope to try to provide portions of an answer to that question.

Conway was born in 1832 to a very wealthy Virginia family in a town called Falmouth, which is still located across from Fredericksburg, about an hour south of Washington, D.C. Fredericksburg was a city that would change hands numerous times during the Civil War. It was located at the headwaters of the Rappahannock River, a river that was navigable from the Chesapeake Bay, all the way to Port Royal and then was not navigable beyond. Therefore, it was an important inland port town, but also Fredericksburg's location on the river, and at such relative close proximity to Washington, D.C., made it a very important crossing point and junction throughout the 18th and into the 19th century. A number of famous Civil War battles—Spotsylvania Court House, Manassas, the Battle of Fredericksburg, the Battle of Marye's Heights—a whole series of Civil War battles were fought in and around that city, partly because it held such a strategic position.

It is also interesting to note that John Wilkes Booth, when he fled Ford's Theatre after assassinating Abraham Lincoln, actually made it only as far as Port Royal, the next town down the river from Falmouth, where he was captured and eventually killed.

In any case, Moncure Conway's father and brothers were slaveholders and in most respects, they were Southern sympathizers. That will, of course, become our first point of distinction from most of the Transcendentalists. What is important to our understanding of Moncure, however, was that his mother was clearly much more liberal in her thinking than his father, and Moncure, particularly as he grew up, seemed to side much more with the liberal aspects of his mother's thinking. Transcendentalism, at this time in the 1830s and even into the 1840s, was little known and even less of an influence in the southern states. I think the first thing to say is partly because agriculture so dominated industry—I will come back to that point— but also because conservative religious denominations still dominated liberal denominations.

As we have seen, part of what allowed the Transcendentalists ways of thinking to take hold in New England, especially in that area around Boston and Concord, was the desire on the part of many individuals to separate their theology from that strict fundamentalist interpretation of those early New England Calvinists. Most people in the South at this time were willing to stick with their more literal interpretations of the Bible, and we did not see the same kind of questioning of religious belief that was going on in the North.

The other important element of this development is that the agricultural lifestyle caused many more people to be involved, not only slaves, but also slaveholders, in the very process of producing their sustenance and it allowed much less time for developments either of intellectual activity or of academic inquiry of certain kinds. It is worth noting that while the College of William & Mary had been founded in the 17th century, the University of Virginia, just down the road from Fredericksburg, would not even be founded until 1819, just a few years before Moncure's birth.

Moncure attended Dickinson College in Pennsylvania at the time it was still a Methodist school. Dickinson College has an important place in my own history because it is the institution at which I have been teaching for almost the last 20 years. When I wander through the halls of the building, East College, in which my office is located, I often think of Conway who actually had his residence there and would have had many of his classes there since that building was built in the 1830s. Our oldest building on the Dickinson Campus is Old West—designed by Benjamin Latrobe, who designed the U.S.

Capitol—and that was the only other building in existence at Dickinson College at the time. Therefore, between those two buildings, we have all of the spaces that Conway would have occupied during his college education. For this reason, as well as his connection to Transcendentalism, I have always had a soft spot for Moncure's life and history.

It is clear that he was first exposed to the ideals of Emerson at Dickinson; in fact, he even recounts the year 1847, when he read Emerson for the first time. I have spent a number of hours in the Dickinson College library trying to discover if we have an edition of Emerson that goes back as far as Conway's attendance and apparently there is one that is just about fifteen years too late to have been the one that Conway actually read.

At this time it is fair to say that the South was extremely suspicious of Transcendentalism, by the late 1840s now, and especially of Emerson. Let me try and explain why. Emerson had a series, as we have seen, of egalitarian ideas that had to be perceived as a direct threat to an aristocratic society, which drew the strong distinction between land-owning aristocrats and people of lower social classes. But even more of a threat, Emerson's egalitarianism had to be even more of a threat to a slaveholding society that although on the one hand it acknowledged a pastoral myth, part of the story in the south of America was that it sought and described a pastoral ideal for American life and culture. But that myth could never be fully democratic if we had large numbers of people having to work at extremely menial and manual levels of labor in order to produce the agricultural crops that would support a few very wealthy aristocrats at the top of the social scale. I think there are aspects both of the agrarian element in the South, and also the slave-owning aspect of the South, that meant there would be conscious and outright resistance to Transcendentalism as soon as these ideas came further south.

Conway actually wrote a youthful letter to Emerson in which he claimed to be what he called "A Natural Radical—to whose soul Radicalism is as air to a bird." Yet another organic metaphor, "My soul is radical" in the same way that air is natural to a bird. Also a very prophetic utterance, as we will see. In this same early letter to Emerson, Moncure lamented his upbringing among conservative

Southerners and argued that he wanted a very different life for himself.

He went north after his graduation from Dickinson—and a short period of time as a circuit-riding Methodist minister—to enter Harvard Divinity School, from which he graduated in 1854. What had actually happened formally is that after his period of time as a Methodist circuit rider—as they were called, who went from church to church to give sermons—his own religious doubts and his own increasing religious liberalism caused him to become a Unitarian. That same shift that we saw in so many of the New England Transcendentalists, here happening to Conway, even in the area around southern Pennsylvania, where he was a circuit rider.

He soon met Emerson once he went to Cambridge, Massachusetts and they became close friends. From that moment on, he would describe Emerson as his "spiritual father," but the relationship between them came to be actually quite close. He also met Bronson Alcott and Thoreau and almost immediately became an abolitionist under the influence not only of Theodore Parker, but also William Lloyd Garrison, who by that time was probably the most widely known abolitionist in the country.

He knew Thoreau quite well and gave a famous and often-quoted description of Thoreau that I think tells us something not only about Thoreau, but also about Conway. Here is the quote describing Thoreau:

> Like the pious Yogi, so long motionless whilst gazing on the sun that knotty plants encircled his neck and the cast snake-skin his loins, and the birds built their nests on his shoulders, this poet and naturalist, by equal consecration a part of the field and the forest.

This remarkable image of Thoreau, sitting still for so long, as one of our earlier passages suggested, that the plants have actually grown around him and the snake has actually had time to shed its skin in his lap. It is a wonderful combination of a light touch of satire with this very honest appreciation.

Conway became the minister of the First Unitarian Church in Washington, D.C., but interestingly, in terms of his own history and the history of that denomination, he was soon dismissed for preaching against slavery as being immoral. Here, in a Unitarian church as far south as Washington, even to preach that slavery was immoral could be seen as grounds for dismissal as the preacher.

He took a new wife with him to Falmouth, Virginia, but she scandalized his entire family when she first embraced, and then went on to kiss, a young female slave. Here again, we have a wonderful anecdote that suggests the kinds of conflicts in Conway's life—bringing his wife home, she very naturally, being from further north, embraces and then kisses a slave who is a member of the household, and she is almost banished from the family as a result.

Conway's reputation grew fairly quickly to the point where he was well enough known by the Civil War to actually visit the White House in an early effort to convince Lincoln that the only solution would be for Lincoln to free all of the slaves. This was well enough before the Emancipation Proclamation that Lincoln, in effect, said that he could not agree with Conway's advice and so having failed to convince Lincoln at this time, Conway actually left Washington, went back to Virginia and led his own family's slaves to freedom in Ohio. He was involved directly again, in a form of abolitionist activity that involved, in his case, his own family.

It was also the case that not long after this period of time, around the Civil War, Conway became dissatisfied not only with life in the South, but also with life in America, and upon the end of the Civil War he moved to England. I think, from looking at his readings, especially his autobiography, we might say that when he left for England, Conway felt too Southern to be a full Northerner when he spent time in and around Boston. But he felt far too Northern, based on his education and his commitment to Transcendentalist principles, to ever feel at home in the South. Partly for those reasons, he left for England.

In London, he continued his career as a social activist and it is fair to say most fully developed his career as a public speaker. As I have said, he soon came to know a wide range of England's most influential people at the time, including Dickens, Carlyle and Darwin. He visited Charles Darwin at Darwin's home at Down House outside of London and he noted after that visit—a quote from his autobiography, Darwin "expressed satisfaction that I had been able to derive from evolution, the hopeful religion set forth in my discourse, but I remember that he did not express agreement with it."

Part of the problem in England, by the 1860s and 1870s, was the question about whether Darwin's theory of evolution could be brought into sync with any form of theological thinking and clearly here we see Conway struggling to make that attempt and Darwin's not being convinced.

He was able to continue all of his freethinking ideas—human equality, women's suffrage, complete religious freedom or even freedom from religion—in what we would have to see as the more accepting and conducive climate of England. If he could find room for freethinking in the North that he couldn't find in the South, he could certainly even find a wider acceptance of his ideas in the open atmosphere in England, especially in the areas around London.

He wrote a series of influential biographies of Emerson, in which he was willing to discuss his own growing disagreements with his master, his spiritual father. He also wrote a well received biography of Nathaniel Hawthorne and another of Thomas Paine; all of these biographies helped to contribute to that Transcendentalist cult of the individual, that idea that one of the best ways to study history would be by studying the biographies of great individuals. That was an idea that Emerson, you may remember, had also derived and expanded from Thomas Carlyle.

What eventually happened to Conway in terms of his home was that he traveled back and forth between England and America. I do not think he ever felt quite at home in either place, so in a way, similar to not feeling at home in either the North or the South. Conway was a ruthless individual who I suspect, when he was in England, felt more like an American, and then when he was in America, felt like he needed some of that fresh air of England.

After the end of the Civil War, it was clear that he had not felt comfortable in any part of the United States. I think by the 1870s and 1880s, it is fair to say that his ideas were even too liberal and perhaps too forward looking to allow him to feel comfortable in either Europe or America. I will explain what I mean by that in a moment.

He ended up in Paris, which may be the last refuge of all freethinkers, where he actually died in 1907. That makes him one of the few Transcendentalists who literally, in terms of his biological life, brought the ideas of the Transcendentalist into the 20th century. As did Emerson and Fuller, this also means I think—this history means—that he contributed to what we could call the internationalization of these Transcendentalist ideas, by traveling widely overseas and by publishing a number of works that were as widely read in Europe as they were in North America. In 1864, he published *Testimonies Concerning Slavery*, one of his powerful abolitionist works. He also published *The Sacred Anthology: A Book of Ethical Scriptures* in 1874. You may remember that the Transcendentalists were drawn to this idea of ethical scriptures that might be drawn from any religious tradition, but could teach all of us things we needed to know about how to be good. And finally, he wrote an autobiography that appeared three years before his death and which has been perhaps the best source of information about his life.

Conway, as Emerson and others before him, eventually found himself leaving organized religion altogether. But even more than most of the other Transcendentalists, Conway ended up favoring a secular and almost a scientific version of spirituality, which goes back to that quotation from his afternoon with Darwin at Down House. As he wrote in a powerful and, you will appreciate, controversial passage, after giving up on the idea of a personal God in any way, "Eyes turned from phantom gods have caught glimpses of a divine life in the evolution of nature, and the mystical movement at the heart of man."

That was from an essay called "Christianity," published in the mid-1870s in which Conway tried to define his own sense of what it might mean to be a Christian, but also suggested how his own ideas took him away from what he, here, describes as "phantom gods." Yet he still claims that even in the ideas of evolution, he finds what he wants to call a "divine life" and a "mystical movement" at the heart of human beings.

Conway's personal abandonment of religion was spurred in part by the death of his own young son, appropriately named Emerson. There is an interesting parallel here to Darwin's own religious disillusionment, which was brought about by his 10-year-old daughter's death. There was a phenomenon that was not uncommon to a number of these Victorians; they would lose a child and the loss of that child would become the reason for their final unwillingness to ascribe any general principle of goodness behind the Universe. "How could anything like a good God allow my innocent 10-year-old child to die?" is basically the way both Darwin, and later Conway, expressed this difficulty.

Conway, in a similar way, ended up believing that Emerson was overly optimistic and that what we would have to call a hard-nosed scientific rationalism was the only mode of thought that would move us close to the truth about the Universe. Admittedly for Conway, this rationalism could include something called divinity, but it was a divinity very much to be found in the truths of science. Not many individuals at his time, or perhaps even subsequently, have been willing to push the logic of their skepticism as far as Conway's really quite strict materialism. But such thinking and such a willingness to pull spirituality this far from organized religion would become a model for many 20th-century intellectuals.

Conway's influence remained widespread, even after he came to be acknowledged as such a radical freethinker. Obviously ideas such as this, that the truths of the universe could be found only through science, or that if there was something called spirituality, it had to be able to be linked to the material circumstances surrounding us. Those were ideas that would have certainly been seen as radical free thought at any time in the 19th century. What is interesting is the number of people who continued to ally themselves with Conway or to suggest his influence on them. For example, Dickinson College took up a collection of funds to build a building on the campus in honor of Conway after his death in 1907 and here is the list of individuals who contributed: Mark Twain, Walt Whitman, Elizabeth Cady Stanton and Andrew Carnegie. Therefore if, upon his death, he was still willing to draw support from an august group of Americans such as that, it is clear that his influence extended in lots of directions. It is also, to me, always a surprise that with a list such as that he is not better known today than perhaps he is. I think it is because, as I have suggested, a lot of his writings at the time were more contemporary and perhaps have not stood the test of time. I would probably recommend his autobiography as the best source for beginning to gain information or a wider knowledge about him.

In fact, Andrew Carnegie, among many other notables, actually attended Conway's memorial service, which was held in New York City in 1907. There is, as I have suggested earlier in this lecture, one important memorial to Conway. The building at Dickinson College unfortunately has been torn down and has been replaced without his name. But Conway Hall in Red Lion Square in London is a building, a beautiful edifice in fact, not far from central London, founded by the South Place Ethical Society in the early-20th century, and it is a building that remains, in lots of ways, a powerful tribute to his memory. Here a whole range of individuals come to speak, to lecture; there are musical performances; there are poetry readings. For example, when the author, Salman Rushdie, was under the *fatwa,* established by the Ayatollah because of the controversy surrounding his novel, *The Satanic Verses*, one of the first places that Salman Rushdie came out of hiding and spoke in London was at Conway Hall. The Hall announces on its website that it still sets out to encourage the sort of free speech and progressive thought that were once advocated by Moncure Conway.

With that, we will turn to an interesting group of Transcendentalists that I like to think of as the eccentrics.

Lecture Sixteen
Transcendental Eccentrics

Scope:

Transcendentalism produced more than its share of eccentrics, and some of their viewpoints helped to create a uniquely American version of eccentricity. Thoreau himself seemed very eccentric to many of those in and around Concord. The younger William Ellery Channing, nephew of Dr. Channing, was perhaps most famous for his important friendships: Emerson, the Alcott patriarch, Nathaniel Hawthorne, and Thoreau all counted him as a boon companion and sparkling conversationalist. Channing lived in a rustic cottage in the woods 10 years before his more illustrious friend Thoreau did so at Walden. The younger Channing married Margaret Fuller's sister, but he was unable to remain married to her or to raise his five children by her. He went on to write one of the first biographies of Thoreau. Our final eccentric, Jones Very, was a curious but impassioned zealot. Some said that he was chosen by God (especially Very himself); others said that he was insane. What cannot be doubted is that Very produced poems and other writings that helped to solidify a link between independent or artistic thinking and eccentric behavior.

Outline

I. A certain idea of freedom linked to Transcendentalism brought with it the freedom to act in ways that others might not find normal or socially acceptable.

    A. Thoreau was no doubt the most well known of the Transcendentalist eccentrics and was often described that way by others.

        1. What people seemed to mean by *eccentric* was that Thoreau was not fit for a normal life in polite society, as we have already noted.

        2. The *Boston Atlas and Daily Bee* described him as follows: "Mr. Thoreau is an eccentric individual, having lived until within a short time, in a hut, in the woods, between Concord and Lincoln." Thoreau himself

addressed this view of his life when he wrote in a letter: "You must not blame me if I do talk to the clouds."

3. Such behavior may be good in cases where it produces original ideas or new ways of solving old or intractable problems.

4. The same tendency creates problems when it leads to antisocial, anti-familial actions or a way of life that ultimately does harm to the individual or those around them: criminals, vagrants, the mentally ill.

B. Beyond Thoreau, one recent critic has noted that Alcott and the less well-known Orestes Brownson eventually "mortgaged their reputations to a succession of eccentric causes."

C. This is part of a tradition that goes back as far as Socrates's notion of the "divine madness" of the poet, an idea that includes thinkers and writers ranging from St. Francis of Assisi and William Blake to Albert Einstein and Andy Warhol.

II. William Channing (1817–1901) was the nephew of his more famous namesake, Dr. William Ellery Channing, the former usually called "Doctor" Channing; the latter, simply "Ellery."

A. His mother died when he was five. The scholar Ann Woodlief has suggested that this loss may be the source of the depression, melancholy, and loneliness that affected him in later years; we should recall the number of orphans and widowed individuals of this era.

1. Channing was undisciplined from childhood, and he dropped out of Harvard and then failed once again as a law student.

2. From an early age, however, he pointed out each flower, bird, or insect that he observed in the natural world around him. Everyone from Thoreau to the elder Henry James commented on the precise care and attentiveness of his observations. He examined objects with an almost childlike intensity.

3. He was unable to provide, financially or emotionally, for his wife (the sister of Margaret Fuller) or their five children. She left him and sent the children to relatives at

a time when such a marital separation was almost unheard of among members of polite society.

B. Channing sent many of his curious poems to Emerson to publish in *The Dial*. Emerson did so and consistently defended Channing's strange poetry against the criticism of others.

   1. Thoreau called the lyric poems "sublime-slipshod," by which he seems to have meant vaguely abstract and technically careless.

   2. Edgar Allan Poe was even harsher in his review: "His book contains about sixty-three things, which he calls poems, and which he no doubt seriously supposes them to be. They are full of all kinds of mistakes, of which the most important is that of their having been printed at all."

   3. Nevertheless, the rhetoric of some of his poems can sound very modern, almost an anticipation of the conversational and direct diction of Ezra Pound or the young T. S. Eliot. Here is a quote from "Gifts":

> A dropping show of spray,
> Filled with a beam of light,—
> The breath of some soft day,—
> The groves by wan moonlight,—
> > Some rivers flow,
> > Some falling snow,
> Some bird's swift flight.

   4. There are techniques here that remind us of the French Symbolists, the Modernists, and even the voice of a great deal of contemporary poetry: compressed, personal, meditative.

C. In 1839, Channing traveled to Illinois, where he lived in a tiny dirt-floored hut and farmed a small plot with his own hands. This effort to get back to the land would later inspire his more famous friend.

   1. Ten years after this time as a hermit, Thoreau and Channing took a trip to Cape Cod, the first of a number of such trips. He was probably Thoreau's best friend.

   2. In fact, Channing later wrote a letter to Thoreau in which he said: "I see nothing for you on this earth but that field which I once christened 'Briars'; go out upon that, build yourself a hut, and there begin the grand process of devouring yourself alive. I see no alternative, no other hope for you."

3. When Thoreau uses the anonymous initial C. in his *Journal* he is apparently referring to Channing, who is also likely to be part of the composite figure of "the Poet" referred to in *Walden*: an idealistic, otherworldly, starry-eyed dreamer.

4. Channing was not widely known for his poetry, then or now, but he was significantly the first person to write a book-length biography of Thoreau; *Thoreau, the Poet-Naturalist* (1873) became his most important and widely read work and inspired interest in, and subsequent writing about, his more famous eccentric friend.

5. Channing lived on until 1901, like Conway, bringing the direct influence of New England Transcendentalism into the dawn of the 20th century.

III. Our final eccentric, Jones Very (1813–1880), was one of those divinely inspired religious madmen who appear at certain points in history and produce a powerful affect on people around them.

A. Very moved early in life into the circle of New England intellectuals of the period.

1. He was born in Salem to first cousins who never married. His mother was an outspoken atheist.

2. He went to Harvard, where he won the Bowdoin Prize two years in a row and drew praise for his work as a classicist and for his essays on poetry and religious topics.

3. He was powerfully influenced by European Romantic writers and by Shakespeare and, soon after his first reading of *Nature*, by Emerson.

4. Emerson's "Divinity School Address" set forth ideas Very took to heart: "The man who renounces himself, comes to himself," and the poet should make himself into "a newborn bard of the Holy Ghost,—cast behind you all conformity, and acquaint men at first hand with Deity"; this kind of direct witness and mystical nonconformity became Very's goal.

B. In 1838, Very underwent his powerful spiritual rebirth: "In my senior year in college I experienced what is commonly called a change of heart, which tells us that all we have belongs to God and that we ought to have no will of our own."

    1. His crisis and resulting move toward an otherworldly mysticism was so extreme that he was committed for a month to the McLean Asylum for the mentally ill. He said that he had been personally chosen by God.

    2. He had stayed on after graduation at Harvard as a divinity student and tutor of Greek, but by the autumn of 1838, he was encouraging his students that they should "Flee to the mountains, for the end of all things is at hand."

    3. His writings indicate that at times he clearly saw himself as a sort of second coming of a Christ-like divinity:

> I saw on earth another light
> Than that which lit my eye
> Come forth as from my soul within,
> And from a higher sky. ("The Light from Within")

C. He published a book of essays and poems with the encouragement and editorial guidance of Emerson, who supported Very's literary talent, as he did the younger Channing's.

    1. Emerson personally reviewed Very's poems and essays in 1841 in *The Dial*: "The author, plainly a man of a pure and kindly temper, casts himself into the state of the high and transcendental obedience to the inward Spirit. He has apparently made up his mind to follow all its leadings, though he should be taxed with absurdity or even with insanity."

    2. Very also was linked to a strain in Protestant mysticism known as Quietism: "The hand and foot that stir not, they shall find/Sooner than all the rightful place to go."

    3. In his best works, he achieves an almost Eastern annihilation of the personal will that would be echoed in Emerson and Thoreau; his spiritual life required that the individual will be swallowed up by the will of God, an idea that links a kind of ecstatic intensity with Quietist mysticism:

> I saw the spot where our first parents dwelt;
> And yet it wore to me no face of change,
> For while amid its fields and groves I felt
> As if I had not sinned, nor thought it strange.
> ("The Garden")

4. As a writer, he had what many saw as the audacity to assume God's voice or point of view. He wrote hundreds of poems in total, many surrounding his intense conversion or "new birth" but also many after he received permission to preach as a Unitarian in 1843.

5. This form of religious eccentricity remains with us when we think about religious individuals who seem somehow beyond ordinary life. This is a positive idea in the case of John the Baptist or Julian of Norwich, but it is clearly negative in the case of Jim Jones or David Koresh.

6. The general mood of Transcendentalist inquiry often produced this type of intensely personal questioning or transformation of belief. The residual cultural notion is the idea that it is generally acceptable to go your own way as long as your actions do not harm yourself or others.

7. We still debate what constitutes acceptable social behavior, especially when the actions are linked to religious observance or a belief system.

Essential Reading:

McGill, Frederick T., Jr. *Channing of Concord: A Life of William Ellery Channing II.*

Very, Jones. *The Complete Poems.* Ed. Helen R. Deese.

Questions to Consider:

1. What was it about the views of Transcendentalists that led them to attract the attention of people we might think of as eccentrics?

2. Consider the conflict between conformity and nonconformity in American culture; what is it that often draws us to nonconformists?

Lecture Sixteen—Transcript
Transcendental Eccentrics

Hello again. Now we turn to the interesting question of transcendental eccentrics. Transcendentalism produced more that its share of eccentric individuals and a number of their viewpoints helped, I think, to create a uniquely American version of eccentricity. Of course, Thoreau himself must have seemed eccentric to many of those in and around him in Concord and Boston. The younger William Ellery Channing, who was the nephew of Dr. Channing, about whom we learned in an earlier lecture, was perhaps most famous not only for his eccentricity, but also for his important friendships—Emerson, the Alcott patriarch, Nathaniel Hawthorne and Thoreau himself, all counted this Channing as a close companion and a sparkling conversationalist.

Channing actually lived in a rustic cottage in the woods almost ten years before his more illustrious friend, Thoreau, did so at Walden. The younger Channing also married Margaret Fuller's sister, but he was unable to remain married to her or to help raise his five children by her. We will hear more about that later. He did, in any event, go on to write one of the first significant biographies of Thoreau and, in that sense, was important in helping Thoreau gain a wider audience.

Our final eccentric in this lecture had the curious name of Jones Very and he was indeed, a curious, but also very impassioned religious zealot. Some said that he was chosen by God, especially Very himself. Others said that he was probably insane. What cannot be doubted is that Very produced a group of poems and other writings that helped to solidify a clear link between independent, or perhaps artistic thinking, and also eccentric behavior.

I think to begin we should note that a certain idea of freedom, especially personal human freedom, was linked to Transcendentalism and this idea brought with it perhaps, freedom to act in ways that other people might not always find normal or at least socially acceptable. Indeed Thoreau himself was no doubt the most well known of the Transcendentalist eccentrics. In fact, he was often described that way by other people. What these people seemed to mean by "eccentric" in Thoreau's case was that he was not fit for what we might describe as a normal life in polite society, especially at a time when most people were so concerned with appropriate social graces, behaviors that were acceptable to individual social classes and so on.

The Boston *Atlas and Daily Bee*, a local newspaper, described Thoreau as follows, "Mr. Thoreau is an eccentric individual, having lived until within a short time, in a hut, in the woods, between Concord and Lincoln."

Just the activity of living in a hut in the woods was enough to associate Thoreau with the idea of eccentricity. But before we criticize others for this view of Thoreau, we should point out that Thoreau himself addressed this precise view of his life when he wrote in a letter, "You must not blame me if I do talk to the clouds." Of course we know that Thoreau is being satirical here about his own time spent in the natural world, but he clearly is also sensing the impression that his life is having on other people.

If we think about eccentric behavior in general, in almost any society, it is clear that eccentricity may be thought of as good in cases where it produces original ideas or perhaps new ways of solving old or intractable problems. This is often the case when we associate artistic or imaginative thinking with a certain sort of normally unacceptable social behavior. In this regard, the same tendencies can create problems when they lead to what I suppose we would see as anti-social, perhaps anti-familial actions or to a way of life for the individual that ultimately harms that person or perhaps those around them. In this sense of course, we often associate eccentricity with vagrants, perhaps sometimes with criminals and certainly very often with the mildly or more severely mentally ill.

Beyond just Thoreau, one recent writer—about the Transcendentalists—has noted that Bronson Alcott and the less well known Orestes Bronson, another member of the early circle, eventually "mortgaged their reputations to a succession of eccentric causes." In this regard the question is not just does the person behave in ways that are seen as eccentric by those around them, but do they also associate themselves with groups or ideas that seem on the margins or out of the mainstream of society?

This wider idea, I suppose, is part of a tradition that goes back even as far as Socrates and his notion of a "divine madness" that inspires the poet—some sort of a linkage between behavior that seems mad, or on the borders of psychologically acceptable, linked to some sort of divinity or awareness that goes beyond normal behavior. This is an idea that I think would have to be invoked to include individuals, thinkers, writers and religious figures perhaps, ranging from St. Francis of Assisi and the poet, William Blake, all the way in our own time to Albert Einstein whose curious behavior was often noted by those who knew him well, and certainly an artist like Andy Warhol.

Our second Ellery Channing, as I have said, was the nephew of his more famous namesake, Dr. William Ellery Channing. The former is usually called "Doctor" Channing and the latter, his nephew, is usually simply referred to as "Ellery" in order to distinguish the two.

The younger Channing's mother died when he was only five years old and the scholar of Transcendentalism, Ann Woodlief, has suggested that this early loss of his mother may have been a strong contributing factor to the depression, the melancholy and the loneliness that this younger Channing often described affecting him in later years.

I think this is a good point to remind ourselves of the number of orphans that we have seen in this series of lectures and also the number of widowed individuals. There was a very common phenomenon in society—of being a child left with only one, or in some cases, no parents from an early age or a spouse who was left on his or her own far too early in life.

Channing was described as extremely undisciplined from childhood and by the time he reached his late adolescence, he dropped out of Harvard first and then not long after that, failed once again as a law student. From an early age, however, he did—according to those who knew him and spent time with him—observe very carefully every flower, every bird, every insect in the natural world around him. We can see here already what might have drawn him into a close connection with Thoreau. Indeed, everyone from Thoreau to the elder Henry James commented on the extremely precise care and the attentiveness of Channing's observations. He seemed to examine objects with an almost childlike intensity and this reminds us again, I think, of a connection to that idea from Romanticism—very often the child possesses qualities that are lost as the person grows up and becomes more socialized.

As a result of his impractical personality, Channing was unable to provide either financially or emotionally for his wife, as I have said, the sister of Margaret Fuller, about whom we have already heard, or any of their five children. Eventually his wife left him and sent these children to various relatives at a time when such a marital separation was almost unheard of among members of polite or middle class society.

Channing sent many of his curious poems, that he had been writing from an early age, to Emerson to publish in *The Dial* magazine. Emerson did so almost immediately and he consistently defended what seemed to many to be Channing's strange poetry, against the criticisms of most other readers. Even Thoreau called Channing's lyric poems "sublime-slipshod," that is Thoreau's phrase, by which he seems to have meant both vaguely abstract—I suspect that is the reference to sublime, but also technically careless—slipshod in the sense of either tossed off or not following the accepted rules for poetry at the time.

Edgar Allan Poe was much harsher in his own review of Channing's collection of poetry. Here is what Poe had to say:

His book contains about sixty-three things, which he calls poems, and which he no doubt seriously supposes them to be. They are full of all kinds of mistakes, of which the most important is that of their having been printed at all.

Here is Poe being a little more humorous than we ordinarily expect him to be. His problem with Channing I think, relates both to formal rules for poetry, which were still very important at this point in history, and also to the fact that Channing was pushing the boundary, as we will see, for what constituted acceptable subject matter.

It is clear to us now, however, that the rhetoric of some of his poems can actually sound very modern, almost an anticipation of the conversational and the very direct diction, the very straight-forward style of later poets such as Ezra Pound or the young T. S. Eliot. I think, for my purposes, the problem with Channing in his own time is that his poetry anticipated a style and a series of subject matters, particularly common, ordinary events that looked really to the 20th century for the fulfillment of that idea of what might constitute acceptable poems.

Here is a quotation from his poem, "Gifts," that captures this sense I think:

A dropping show of spray,
Filled with a beam of light,—
The breath of some soft day,—
The groves by wan moonlight,—
Some rivers flow,
Some falling snow,
Some bird's swift flight.

What is remarkable here is the understated quality of the verse and the fact that the poet seems to be making little or no comment about the significance of the events he is describing. Instead he is simply allowing experience to stand alone. There are techniques here that will actually remind us of the French Symbolists—much later in the 19th century—of the early Modernists, as I have noted, and even of the voice of a great deal of our own contemporary poetry—compressed, personal and meditative.

Channing traveled to Illinois in 1839, where he lived in a tiny dirt-floored cottage and farmed a small plot with his own hands. This effort, as we might say, to go back to the land would later clearly inspire his more famous friend.

Ten years after his own time as a hermit, Channing actually joined Thoreau for a trip to Cape Cod, the first of a number of such trips. Indeed, a number of commentators both at the time and subsequently, have argued that Channing was probably Thoreau's best friend in the sense of the person who spent most time and perhaps understood Thoreau as well as any other individual.

In fact, after his own sojourn in the wilderness, Channing wrote a letter to Thoreau in which he said this:

I see nothing for you on this earth but that field which I once christened 'Briars'; go out upon that, build yourself a hut, and there begin the grand process of devouring yourself alive. I see no alternative, no other hope for you.

There is another very strong poetic image; you need to "devour yourself alive," clearly Channing was speaking figuratively. But in this remarkable passage we see Channing telling Thoreau quite directly, "go to that place in the woods," that bit of land owned by Emerson, "build yourself a hut and live in the woods as I did." In fact, when Thoreau uses the anonymous initial C. in his *Journal*, he seems clearly to refer to Channing, who is also almost definitely part of the composite figure of the poet that Thoreau often refers to in Walden—an idealistic, otherworldly almost starry-eyed dreamer.

Channing never became widely known for his poetry, either then or now, but he was significantly the first person to write a book-length biography of Thoreau. It was entitled *Thoreau, the Poet-Naturalist*, and was first published in 1873. It immediately became his most important and widely read work, and it inspired a large surge of interest in, and subsequent writing about, his more famous eccentric friend.

It is also worth noting that like Moncure Conway before him, Channing lived on into the 20th century, not dying until 1901, and therefore, helping extend the influence of New England Transcendentalism into the dawn of the 20th century.

Our final eccentric for this lecture for this lecture is Jones Very, one of those divinely inspired religious madmen perhaps, who appear at certain points in history and nevertheless, produce a powerful effect on many of the people around them. Very moved early in his own life into the circle of New England intellectuals that we have been describing in this series of lectures.

He was born in Salem, Massachusetts—again, famous for the witchcraft trials—to first cousins who, perhaps significantly, perhaps not, ever married. It probably is significant that his mother was an outspoken atheist at a time when that word alone could get any individual, much less a woman, into a great deal of trouble.

In any case, Very went to Harvard, where he won the Bowdoin Prize two years in a row, almost the opposite of the younger Channing, and he drew praise for his work both as a classical scholar and for his essays on poetry and on religion. Like so many of the figures we have been discussing, he was powerfully influenced by European Romantic writers and by Shakespeare, and almost immediately, upon his first reading of *Nature*, by Emerson.

In fact, it was Emerson's "Divinity School Address" that set forth a series of ideas that Very took to heart almost immediately. Here is Emerson: "The man who renounces himself, comes to himself," or each poet should make himself into "a newborn bard of the Holy Ghost, cast behind you all conformity, and acquaint men at first hand with Deity." This direct witness of the divine and this mystical nonconformity, this effort not to conform to social expectations became Very's precise goal.

In 1838, he underwent a powerful spiritual rebirth. Here is Very describing the experience, "In my senior year in college I experienced what is commonly called a change of heart, which tells us that all we have belongs to God and that we ought to have no will of our own."

This, of course, is not unusual as conversion language for any number of religious individuals, especially mystics, who claim a specific moment in their life at which they decide they have to renounce most of the things of the world and take on a separate mantle that will have them more closely associated with the divine force that controls the Universe.

For Jones Very, however, this precipitated a serious crisis and a move toward what we have to call an other-worldly mysticism that was so extreme that he was actually committed for a month to the McLean Asylum for the mentally ill. Those around him decided that the force and the intensity with which he had felt this conversion experience made it impossible for him to continue any longer in normal society, so he actually spent a month in an asylum. All during this time, he continued to say that he had been personally chosen by God for a purpose that was still waiting to be fulfilled.

He had actually stayed on, after his first graduation from Harvard, as a divinity student and as a tutor of Greek, but by the autumn of 1838, he was encouraging his students in ways that caused serious concern for other people. He told his students that they needed to "Flee to the mountains, for the end of all things is at hand." This kind of immediate apocalyptic language clearly got him into trouble, not only with Harvard authorities, but also with those who were concerned for his sanity.

His writings actually indicate that at times he saw himself almost as a second coming of a very Christ-like divinity. Here is a passage from one of his poems called "The Light from Within:"

> I saw on earth another light
> Than that which lit my eye
> Come forth as from my soul within,
> And from a higher sky.

That sense of being especially privileged to envision that is not vouchsafe to anyone else. Clearly, Very associates with a light that comes from within himself, and he certainly claims that this gives him a vision that other people are not in possession of.

He did go on to publish a book of essays and poems with the encouragement and the editorial guidance of Emerson, who supposed that Very's literary talent was worthy of this recognition, and he supported that talent in the same way that he had done for the younger Channing. In fact, Emerson personally reviewed these poems and essays in 1841 in an edition of *The Dial*. Here is what Emerson had to say; listen carefully, we will see how Emerson himself is commenting on the question of his subject's sanity:

The author, plainly a man of a pure and kindly temper, casts himself into the state of the high and transcendental obedience to the inward Spirit. He has apparently made up his mind to follow all its leadings, though he should be taxed with absurdity or even with insanity.

Absurdity or insanity, Emerson says, are the possibilities for where these thoughts may lead. Of course, what may be most significant in that passage is Emerson's willingness to call this inspiration—in Emerson's phrase again—"transcendental obedience to the inward Spirit." That sounds like a good thing, but if it leads to absurdity or even insanity, it clearly will not be a good thing.

Jones Very has also been linked to a strain in Protestant mysticism that is known and Quietism. That is the view that the mystic needs to separate him or herself almost completely from the noise of society. Here is a passage from his poems that suggests that link, "The hand and foot that stir not, they shall find/Sooner than all the rightful place to go." The hand and the foot should stir not; it is in those moments of quiet stillness that the truth will become apparent.

In his best works, I think it is clear that he achieves an almost Eastern annihilation of the personal will that would, as we have seen, be clearly echoed in Emerson and Thoreau. His spiritual life almost came to require that his individual will be swallowed up by the will of God, by an outside force. And this was an idea that clearly links an ecstatic intensity with this same Quietist mysticism. It seems to be another one of those tensions that appear throughout his poetry and also may suggest the sort of psychological tensions he was undergoing within his own mind.

Here is a poem called "The Garden." It may go without saying that what he is really describing here is the First Garden:

> I saw the spot where our first parents dwelt;
> And yet it wore to me no face of change,
> For while amid its fields and groves I felt
> As if I had not sinned, nor thought it strange.

This is a short passage, but it is rather remarkable for its contents. In the poem, the speaker claims to have seen the Garden of Eden. This may certainly be imagined as a figurative rather than a literal claim, although the mystic, in some sense, always argues that he or she is able to see beyond normal experience. Then he says, "it wore to me no face of change," as though, I have seen this before, as though it is always remained as it was at one point in the past, and I, the poet, now have access to this sight. What is most significant in these lines, I think, is the claim in the final line, when Very says, "As if I had not sinned, nor thought it strange." Here is a remarkable poetic metaphor that basically strips away the fundamental Christian principle of Original Sin and imagines the speaker able to say, "At this moment of inspiration, I suddenly felt a kind of divinity within myself that had washed away this Original stain."

As a writer, it might, by now, be obvious that he had what many saw at the time as a real audacity to assume God's voice, which happens in a number of his poems; he actually ends up speaking in the voice of God or if not God's voice, at least a God-like point of view. He wrote hundreds of poems in total, many of them surrounding his intense moment of conversion or "new birth," but also many more after he received permission to preach as a member of the Unitarian church in 1843. The time of his most intense mental instability did not last very long and by 1843, he was actually accepted as a preaching minister within the Unitarian denomination.

I think what is important about this form of religious eccentricity is that this idea still remains with us when we think about religious individuals who seem somehow to live beyond the limitations of ordinary life. This is clearly a very positive idea in the case of traditional figures such as John the Baptist or historical figures such the great Mystic, Julian of Norwich, but a closely related idea becomes a serious problem and very negative in the case of religious leaders such as Jim Jones or David Koresh. Those are people who claim an intense and very mystical religious experience of some kind that, nevertheless, leads them and/or their followers into serious difficulties, often including the death of a religious cult.

What is important for our lectures is that the general mood of transcendental inquiry often produced this kind of intensely personal questioning, or what we might call this transformation of an earlier belief. I think the residual cultural notion that stays with us is the idea that it is generally acceptable to go your own way as long as your actions, your beliefs and your ideas do not harm yourself or harm others. Of course, it is worth noting that we still debate what constitutes acceptable social action, especially when those actions are linked to religious observances or to a strong belief system.

Now with that look at a number of transcendental eccentrics, we will turn to another idealistic vision—that is the question of the possibility of utopia.

Lecture Seventeen
Transcendental Utopias—Living Experiments

Scope:

Transcendentalism was not simply about those major and minor figures who developed and promulgated its doctrines. It was also about a series of attempts at new ways of living that had a powerful impact on 19th-century thinking. Social instability, as well as the gradual move from agrarian to urban life, led numerous individuals to consider alternative modes of family and social organization. Brook Farm, perhaps the most well known of these experiments, was founded by George Ripley. Bronson Alcott founded Fruitlands and the Temple School, itself a sort of idealized educational plan for living. Of course, Walden Pond is also a new version of a kind of utopia, if we can imagine a utopia of a single individual. But the social experiments of the period also included religious communities and loose linkages of like-minded individuals. The goal was often to find smaller social groupings within the wider society that could produce better methods for sharing property, educating the young, and producing a unified vision of social life. Of course, the idea of utopia goes back to Thomas More and Plato, but 19th-century America contributed its own Transcendentalist versions.

Outline

I. America has been a land of experimental communities, especially during the 19th century. Some background will help make sense of the Transcendentalist versions of this phenomenon.

   A. In England, in 1772, "Mother" Ann Lee was told by God that "a place had been prepared" for her followers in America.

      1. Nine believers broke with the Quakers and founded the United Society of Believers in Christ's Second Appearing, linking such utopian movements historically with the founding of America itself as a new "promised" land.

      2. Mother Ann and her followers built the original Shaker community in America in the rugged wilds of New York

State, in which ecstatic visions led to religious ceremonies of "shaking." We know the Shakers now primarily for their furniture.

3. Celibacy and simplicity of life were the Shakers' foundational beliefs. Many believed that Mother Ann was the female aspect of Christ's bisexual spirit and that, in this sense, Christ had already returned, leading believers to claim that all people were equal, regardless of sex or race.

4. Shakers believed in a universal equality that included non-Christians, African-Americans, and Native Americans, some of whom joined these communities.

5. The Shakers would go on to become one of the most durable communal sects in America, establishing almost 20 communities that included nearly 4,000 members by 1850. Up to 20,000 Americans may have lived in Shaker communities for some period of time.

B. Oneida, founded by John H. Noyes, was another of the most well-known utopian communes in American history.

1. Noyes and his followers shared land and property for approximately three decades, and they lived in a single group marriage that included up to 200 individuals, variously called "free love" or "complex marriage."

2. Resistant to turning former city dwellers into successful agrarian farmers, they established a number of business concerns, the most famous of which evolved eventually into the Oneida flatware company.

C. New Harmony, in both Indiana and Pennsylvania, became another widely influential communal experiment.

1. The community was founded as early as 1804 by George Rapp and later sold to Robert Owen.

2. Owen was a visionary Welsh reformer who thought that society might be perfected on the basis of free public education and the abolition of social classes and personal wealth; the community eventually introduced kindergartens and vocational education.

3. Its members included a wide range of scientists (especially geologists), artists, authors, and teachers. Noted theologian Paul Tillich is buried there.

D. The Nashoba community was perhaps the most directly socialist model for subsequent Transcendentalist experiments at Brook Farm and Fruitlands.

    1. Frances Wright came from a prosperous Scots family and became well known for her essays on social ethics.

    2. While at New Harmony, Wright conceived of a community that might address the wrongs of the slave system. She imagined an environment in which former slaves could become self-reliant through education and so-called "schools of industry" designed to produce funds that could buy freedom and return those who wished to Africa, as Marcus Garvey would advocate later.

    3. In 1826, Wright founded Nashoba, which lasted for four years, in Tennessee, with a handful of whites and 15 free blacks.

    4. The community failed in part because whites remained in control through a system of overseers. Reality did not always live up to such ideals.

II. George Ripley's Brook Farm and Bronson Alcott's Fruitlands became the two most successful Transcendentalist attempts at communal living.

    A. Brook Farm was established by former Unitarian minister George Ripley in 1841 in an effort to create a classless society. The goal was to reduce physical labor through shared activity and thereby advance intellectual and spiritual growth.

        1. It began with only 20 members in 1841 but had close to 200 followers by the time it collapsed.

        2. The community succeeded well for a time based on a rational sharing of labor and a link between manual and mental labor.

        3. Members worked in return for food and lodging on the farm; additional income was derived from the well-respected school on site.

        4. Tension emerged by 1844 when the freeform Transcendentalist model clashed with the ideas of Charles Fourier, a French utopian thinker. Ripley had been attracted to Fourier's elaborate organizational structure, based on "phalanxes," by a need for financial support and structured reforms.

5. The uninsured property succumbed to a disastrous fire in 1846 but not before it had become widely known and well respected.

6. Charles Dana, a Brook Farm resident who later became famous as a newspaper editor and secretary of war during the Civil War, said, "In the first place we have abolished domestic servitude. In the second place we have secured thorough education for all. And in the third place we have established justice to the laborer."

B. Brook Farm, more than any other utopian experiment in American history, made an impression on social thinkers and intellectuals.

1. Nathaniel Hawthorne described his experiences there in *The Blithedale Romance*, a novel that satirized the possibility for the success of such communities. He did, however, describe the farm in West Roxbury, just 10 miles from Boston, as "one of the most beautiful places I ever saw in my life, and as secluded as if it were a hundred miles from any city or village," echoing again the American longing for the pastoral.

2. Other notable visitors included Emerson, Margaret Fuller, and Henry James, each of whom was impressed.

3. As Transcendentalists, Ripley and his followers believed deeply in the power of each individual to contribute to creating a better world.

4. Brook Farm, unlike many such communes, preserved a belief in private ownership that did not threaten earlier American ideas about property, the nuclear family, and church or state authority.

C. Fruitlands was Bronson Alcott's idea, an outgrowth of his Temple School.

1. Like Brook Farm, Fruitlands sought a rural retreat that would challenge industrial capitalism, but this dream lasted less than a year, from 1843–1844.

2. Fruitlands turned out to be even less practical than Ripley's experiment: no animal food or animal labor, only the Alcott and Lane families and a handful of eccentrics (a nudist, a cracker-eater), as Louisa May later

recorded in her punning essay, "Transcendental Wild Oats."

   3. When the impractical male idealists would travel to spread the word about their utopian dreams, only the women and children were left behind to work. "They look well in July," Emerson himself said after a visit there: "We shall see them in December."

III. Of course, Thoreau's Walden was also a version of a utopian community, albeit a community of one.

   A. "I never found the companion that was so companionable as solitude."

      1. For Thoreau, the ideal world is a world in which he is in complete control.

      2. He takes his anti-materialism and his antisocial impulses to the extreme.

      3. Something is attractive about this ideal, but when he leaves after two years, Thoreau reminds us that he has many more "lives to lead."

      4. There is a sense in which all utopian communities are experiments, not intended to last forever but, rather, to explore new possibilities for interactions among humans: an America that is not Europe, a new chance.

      5. The sense of a life of limitless possibilities is strong in all these people. When Thoreau said, in *Walden*, "I did not wish to live what was not life, living is so dear," he was expanding on an idea put forth earlier by Emerson: "I had fancied that the value of life lay in its inscrutable possibilities [...] The results of life are uncalculated and uncalculable" ("Experience," 1844).

   B. These reflections on Walden remind us of why so many Americans have been drawn to the ideal of utopian communities, which may not last but have a powerful impact nonetheless.

      1. They often emerge out of the powerful vision of a single individual. They can sometimes be compared to cults.

      2. Many humans have a dream of a perfect world or, at least, a better one.

      3. The ideals set forth by one or shared by some are not shared by all.

4. Over time, such experiments are split apart by jealousy, greed, sexual tensions, or changing priorities.
5. Our own cultural experiments, from the communes of the 1960s to current efforts to define new adult communities, and even revised definitions of the family, are legacies of these idealistic experiments.

Essential Reading:

Francis, Richard. *Transcendental Utopias: Individual and Community at Brook Farm, Fruitlands, and Walden.*

Mandelker, Ira. *Religion, Society, and Utopia in Nineteenth-Century America.*

Questions to Consider:

1. Why have so many people throughout history been drawn to the ideal of utopias or communal living?

2. Why do communal living projects, from the Shakers to Brook Farm to the hippie communes of the 1960s, inevitably fail over time?

Lecture Seventeen—Transcript
Transcendental Utopias—Living Experiments

Now after a group of lectures based on a list of remarkable individuals, we will turn to several lectures built around thematic topics that also cluster around ideas of the Transcendentalists. The first of those will be a consideration of transcendental utopias, which we might call experiments in living. Transcendentalism was clearly not simply about a group of major or minor figures who developed and promulgated a series of doctrines, it was also about a number of significant attempts at new ways of living that had a powerful impact on 19th-century thinking and perhaps even beyond.

Social instability at the time, as well as what we have described as the gradual move from agrarian to urban life, first in New England and eventually in the South, led numerous individuals to consider alternative models of family and of social organization.

Brook Farm was perhaps the most well known of these Transcendentalist experiments. It was founded by George Ripley. Bronson Alcott, as we have already learned, founded his Fruitlands community and also the Temple School, which I think we can see as itself, an idealized educational plan for a better way of living. Of course, I like to say that Walden Pond itself is also a new version of utopia, if we can stretch the idea of utopia far enough to imagine utopia of a single individual, Thoreau there by himself.

But the social experiments of this period also included a series of religious communities and looser linkages of like-minded individuals, as we will see. The goal was often to find smaller social groups within the wider society that could produce better methods for sharing property, educating the young and often producing a more unified vision of social life. Of course the wider idea of utopia goes back to Thomas More and even to Plato's *Republic*. But 19th-century America contributed its own Transcendentalist versions.

It is fair to say that America has been a land of experimental communities, I think especially during the 19th century. Some background in a number of these efforts will help to make sense for us of the Transcendentalist versions of this phenomenon. Let us begin in England in 1772, when a woman who would come to be known eventually as "Mother" Ann Lee was told, she claimed, directly by God that, as she said, "a place had been prepared" for her and for her followers in America. It only took nine believers breaking away from the Quaker denomination to found a group that came to be known and United Society of Believers in Christ's Second Appearing. Even the name of this group links such utopian movements historically, with the founding of America, within the same decade as a new and certainly a "promised" land.

This group, as you may have already guessed, built the original Shaker community in America in the rugged wilds of New York State. In their denomination a series of ecstatic visions led the members of the parish to an experience that came to be known as "shaking." These were simply religious ceremonies in which the worshippers would move, sometimes mildly and sometimes more violently, in ways that some compared to dancing and others described as a phenomenon of losing all self-control. Of course, it is the case that we now know the Shakers perhaps primarily for their furniture, rather than for the details of their religious observances.

The foundational beliefs of the Shaker community were celibacy—an interesting aspect of a number of utopian religious experiments—and probably more important, the idea of simplicity of life. Many of the followers believed that Mother Ann herself was what they described as the female aspect of Christ's own bisexual spirit; in any case, a spirit that included male and female. In that sense, the more extreme Shaker members claimed that Christ had already returned to Earth. But this notion that somehow God on Earth had both a male and female aspect led almost all Shaker believers to claim that people were equal, regardless of their gender and regardless of their race. This Shaker belief in a universal equality that included non-Christians, African-Americans and Native Americans led members of all of these minority communities to join some of the Shaker groups.

Indeed the Shaker communities would go on to become one of the most durable communal sects in America. They established almost 20 communities that included roughly 4,000 members by the middle of the 19th century. It is estimated by historians of the sect that up to 20,000 Americans may have lived in Shaker communities for some period of time.

Our second communal experiment, Oneida, was founded by John H. Noyes, and it became another of the most well known utopian communes in American history. The Oneida membership shared land

and all of their property for approximately three decades, and somewhat more controversially, they lived in a single group marriage that included up to some 200 individuals. This original practice of theirs, this reorganization of family and sexual life, was variously called "free love" or "complex marriage."

They had a strong resistance to the idea of turning former city dwellers into agrarian farmers. A lot of these utopian experiments had a pastoral impulse, but in the case of Oneida, their view that it was more beneficial to establish business concerns in which their members could actually produce their material well being without simply having to live off of the land. Indeed, the most famous of these mercantile experiments evolved into the Oneida silverware or flatware company.

New Harmony, our third experiment, at sites in both Indiana and Pennsylvania, became another widely influential attempt at reorganizing social life. It was founded in 1804 by George Rapp but was later sold to the much more famous and well known Robert Owen. Owen was a clearly visionary Welsh reformer who thought that all of society could be perfected on the basis of the idea of free public education for all individuals and the abolition of any kind of social class and all personal wealth. This was a kind of absolutist socialism that Owen advocated.

The New Harmony community was directly connected with the introduction of kindergartens, another idea that we have seen linked to transcendental thinking and also the important idea of vocational education, of practical sorts of training. Its members included a wide range of scientists for a number of reasons, especially geologists, but also artists, authors and teachers. Of all of these communities, New Harmony perhaps, had the most intellectual aspect. In fact, the noted theologian, Paul Tillich, is actually buried at the Indiana site.

For our purposes, the Nashoba community was perhaps the most directly socialist model for subsequent Transcendentalist experiments at Brook Farm, and later at Fruitlands. Nashoba was founded by Frances Wright, a woman who came from a prosperous Scottish family, and became well known early in her adult life for essays she had written on the concept of social ethics. She had actually lived for a time at New Harmony, and it was there that Wright conceived of a community whose especial goal might be to address the wrongs of slavery. What she imagined was an environment in which former slaves could become self-reliant through education and what she called "schools of industry." These were designed partially to produce funds that could buy freedom for former slaves or buy freedom while these individuals were still slaves and could also produce funds that would allow those who wished to, to return to Africa, an idea that would later be appropriated by the famous reformer, Marcus Garvey.

In 1826, she finally founded Nashoba, which lasted only four years, in Tennessee, with a handful of white members and fifteen freed blacks. The community succeeded for a period of time, but it failed I think in part, as historians suggest, because whites remained in control through a complex system of overseers. As so often happens in these utopian dreams, reality does not always live up to the initial ideal of the community.

Now let us turn to George Ripley's Brook Farm and Bronson Alcott's Fruitlands, as I have suggested, the two most successful or certainly most well known Transcendentalist attempts at forms of communal living.

Brook Farm was initially established by the former Unitarian minister—another one of those ministers who felt forced to leave the pulpit—George Ripley, in 1841. His initial effort seems to have been motivated by a desire to create a classless society. The goal was also to reduce physical labor through shared activity of the membership, and thereby, advance intellectual and spiritual growth. There we should hear the echo of an idea we have already discussed in relation to Alcott. "We will share our labor, and therefore that will give us more time to develop our intellects."

Brook Farm began with only 20 members in 1841. But it had close to 200 followers by the time it collapsed. You will see why I choose that word "collapsed." The community succeeded very well for a time, based on this principle of a rational sharing of labor and a link between manual and mental labor, the idea that intellectuals could be usefully employed in physical activities and that anyone engaged in farming or physical labor should also be reading books and discussing important ideas.

The membership of Brook Farm worked in return for their food and lodgings on the farm, and additional income was derived from a well respected school that developed on the site. By 1844 however, tensions started to emerge in this community when what we might call the free-form Transcendentalist model began to clash with the ideas of Charles Fourier, a French utopian thinker, to whom we have already referred in an earlier lecture. Ripley had actually been attracted to Fourier's elaborate organizational structure, based on a concept called "phalanxes." These were strictly organized barracks that almost resembled some sort of Spartan organization of individual members into smaller units. What happened was that Ripley had felt the need both to raise funds for the community and to impose some structured reforms, but as so often happens, once he became influenced by the ideas of this outside thinker, members of the community started to disagree with him.

The uninsured property actually succumbed to a devastating fire in 1846, but not before many people had visited or been associated with the community and it had become widely known. As Charles Dana, a Brook Farm resident, who later became famous as a newspaper editor, and eventually as secretary of war during the Civil War said, "In the first place, we have abolished domestic servitude. In the second place, we have secured thorough education for all and in the third place we have established justice to the laborer." Although the community only lasted for a few years, there is Dana, willing to say that it had at least succeeded in establishing models that could free people from domestic labor, servitude, education for everyone and a form of justice to people who did the work.

Brook Farm I think, more than any other utopian experiment perhaps in American history, made a direct impression on social thinkers and on intellectuals. Nathaniel Hawthorne for example, described his experiences there in *The Blithedale Romance*, a novel which ultimately satirizes the possibility for the permanent, long-term success of such a community. However, here is his description of the farm in West Roxbury, just 10 miles outside of Boston. Hawthorne said, "It was one of the most beautiful places I ever saw in my life, and as secluded as if it were a hundred miles from any city or village." There is a quote that, once again, echoes that American longing for the idea of the pastoral, for some sort of escape from the pressures of urban life that would be an improvement for families and for social organization.

Other notable visitors to Brook Farm included Emerson himself, Margaret Fuller and Henry James, each one of whom was impressed and described the success that had been achieved there. As Transcendentalists, Ripley and his followers believed deeply in the power of every individual to contribute not only to self-improvement, but also to creating a better world. Brook Farm, unlike many such communities, preserved a belief in private ownership. It was not fully socialist in terms of the idea of complete sharing of property, and I think that was important because that idea did not threaten the earlier American idea about the value of personal property or the nuclear family or even perhaps church and state authority. What Brook Farm seemed to accomplish was a balancing between the rights of the individual, especially for private property, and a more communal experience of living.

Fruitlands, as we have already noted, was Bronson Alcott's idea, in many ways an outgrowth of his Temple School. Like Brook Farm, Fruitlands sought a rural retreat that might challenge industrial versions of capitalism and urban living, but unfortunately this idealistic dream lasted less than a year, from 1843 until only 1844.

Fruitlands, as we might expect, turned out to be even less practical than Ripley's experiment. There was to be no animal food consumed or animal labor of any kind. In fact, only the Alcott family and friends of theirs, the Lane family, along with a handful of other eccentrics—one of whom was a nudist, one of whom ate only crackers—became the membership of this community. Louisa May recorded these eccentrics in her punning essay, "Transcendental Wild Oats," which was her version to recount, in satirical form, both the pros and cons of this kind of idealistic experiment.

When the impractical male idealists would travel around and spread the word about their utopian dreams, as Louisa May told us, only the women and the children were left behind to do all of the hard work. Emerson himself visited Fruitlands and left a very telling comment about his experience there. He said, "They look well in July; we shall see them in December." Clearly Emerson knew that once the weather took a turn for the worse, a community like this might be in difficulty.

Of course I also think it is worth noting that Thoreau's Walden is itself a version of a utopian community, albeit a community of only one person. But let me remind you of an important quote from

Walden; here is what Thoreau said, "I never found the companion that was so companionable as solitude." Once again, we see Thoreau's remarkable ability to marshal his own rhetoric in the service of one of his central ideas: "I feel more comfortable and more companioned when I am alone," he argues, "Than I do in the presence of any other person that I have met." Now as often happens in Thoreau's writing, I think he is exaggerating to some extent. But he is trying to make once again, a very Transcendentalist connection between the value of self-conscious self-awareness—as we might now say, getting in touch with oneself—and these important wider truths that are going to come to us as a result of the time that we spend on our own.

In this sense I think that Thoreau's utopian ideal is almost linked to the notion that modern people in the increasingly industrial and materialized world that he feels around him, in a sense, find themselves cut off from some of the sources of their own strength. Put that individual back in touch with himself or herself, and he or she will actually benefit in ways that could not happen under any other circumstances. This goes back to that idea that we mentioned in an earlier lecture about Walden actually being a state of mind, as much as it is a physical place.

For Thoreau, in that sense, the ideal world may also be a world in which he is in complete control, and perhaps in that sense, this is not as positive a state of being. He does certainly take his own version of anti-materialism and what some of his critics have seen as his anti-social impulses to a certain extreme. Something is clearly attractive about this ideal, certainly to Thoreau and perhaps to many of us. But even Thoreau himself, when he leaves Walden after only two years there reminds us, as he says, that he has many more "lives to lead," an idea that there may not be only one solution to the problems of living often addressed by these utopian experiments.

I suspect there is a sense in which all utopian communities are experiments indeed, that they are not intended to last forever. People often criticize utopias and say, "Well that experiment at Fruitlands only lasted less than a year." I think if we consider the purposes of these efforts, they are really designed to explore new sets of possibilities and interactions among humans and I think this takes us back to an important idea about the founding of America—what Americans wanted was an America that was not Europe, as we have seen. They wanted a new chance, and very often this idea of a new chance becomes manifested in experimental ideas about reorganizing society.

The sense of a life of limitless possibilities is strong in all of these people. What they really seem to want is the opportunity to fulfill their innate potential to the greatest extreme possible. When Thoreau, for example, said in *Walden*, "I did not wish to live what was not life, living is so dear." He is clearly expanding on an earlier idea made by Emerson, "I had fancied that the value of life lay in its inscrutable possibilities ... The results of life are uncalculated and uncalculable."

Let us pay a moment's attention to that powerful language: "I did not wish to live what was not life." That's Thoreau—why not, because living is so dear. There is a sense of the valuation of life and that reminder that the mass of men, as he says, "are leading lives of quiet desperation." "I want something better, I want something more." If we link that then, to Emerson's quote, "I had fancied that the value of life lay in its inscrutable possibilities." Life has unknown possibilities, "uncalculable," Emerson said. There are things we cannot even know or imagine about the potentials of our own lives unless we are willing to take chances, experiment with the ways we live and perhaps reconsider the status quo. I think in many ways those two quotes help to create a context for many of these experiments in living.

These reflections on Walden and on these other communities remind us why so many Americans have been drawn to the ideal of a utopia—an ideal which may not last but which, I think, it is important to remind ourselves, may still have powerful impact nevertheless.

Let us also take a minute to consider both the pros and cons of why these communities do not continue over extended periods of time. Such ideas often emerge out of the powerful vision of a single individual. If we wanted to take that idea to its negative extreme, we could say that utopian alternatives can sometimes be compared to cults. One person has a powerful vision, other people are caught up in the enthusiasm of that idea, and then that group of people separates themselves from society. Of course, many human beings have a dream of a perfect world or at least a better world than the one they find themselves in. The ideals set forth by one person or shared by a small group of people however, even if they are extremely positive and optimistic, will not necessarily be shared by everyone.

If we look at the history of communities like this, we often see that over time, these kinds of experiments are split apart by normal human jealousy, by greed—as I have already suggested—over private property and material possessions—what belongs to whom and who has the right to whose property—by sexual tension, which very often enters into such communities, whether they engage in group marriage or whether they retain a more traditional nuclear version of male/female relations, or I think especially over time, by changing priorities. That is to say, the circumstances that confronted the members of Fruitlands, as even Emerson saw in the beautiful summer, were very different from the circumstances when winter came. And as the needs and experiences of the community alter, it is clear that they may need to be willing to shift their priorities.

I think it is the case that our own cultural experiments from the communes of the 1960s, perhaps even to current efforts, to redefine adult communities or educational systems, and even perhaps our revised definitions of the family. What constitutes a family? Which members of a group of related or unrelated people can appropriately be constituted as members of a family? Even these are legacies of the kinds of idealistic experiments that took place among Transcendentalists in the 19th century.

With that, we will turn to another important thematic concern and that is the idea of education.

Lecture Eighteen
Transcendentalism and Education

Scope:

As we have already seen, the link between Transcendentalism and education was a close one. As one scholar has noted, "All of the major transcendentalists—Emerson, Thoreau, Fuller, Palmer, Alcott, Brownson, Very and more—spent years in the classroom as teachers, and all had found traditional education to be inadequate and stultifying." A number of the leading Transcendentalists were teachers or educators, either briefly or for most of their careers. Others, such as Emerson, had a direct influence on important educational reformers. The very notion of education, not only of children but of all the masses of undereducated Americans in the 19th century, was at the heart of one strain of Transcendentalism. Education at this time was not just a function of public or private schools but also of the pulpit, the public lecture hall, the experimental community, and private tutors. Indeed, the transmission of ideas from one mind to another was at the center of a range of revolutionary ideas from Brook Farm to Alcott's Temple School and down to current ideas about the need for ongoing educational reform and lifelong learning.

Outline

I. Education was central to Transcendentalism for numerous reasons.

    A. Education was fundamentally about the way ideas came into, and remained active within, the mind.

        1. Was the mind passive, a mirror on reality, as most of history had assumed?

        2. Or was the mind active, Romantic, organic, a part of the actual process of understanding, as Kant had argued?

        3. For Transcendentalists, all minds were active creators of their experience; this idea contributed to a democracy of thought in which each person was a potential creative artist or social reformer.

    B. Education was always a social issue, linked directly to the organization of groups of humans into a society.

1. Who was entitled to receive an education? Who decided? Public or private? Church supported or state supported?
2. Who provided the education, and what qualifications were required for teachers?
3. Was the purpose of education liberal, or practical, or both?
4. Even in Europe, the idea of general public education for the masses was still new in the 19th century.

C. Transcendentalist ideas about education were always progressive.
   1. Emerson and Thoreau, like Alcott and Peabody, gave credit to the young for the value of their innocence, their intuitive insights, and their inherent wisdom, unlike almost all earlier views of children.
   2. A key source for Transcendentalist ideas about education was the Swiss humanitarian and educator Johann Pestalozzi (1746–1827), who followed Rousseau and believed in the "inner dignity of each child."
   3. Important educators subsequently influenced by Transcendentalist ideals included Francis Parker (1837–1902), who developed the primary school and the P.T.A. and whom John Dewey (1859–1952) called the "father of progressive education," and Dewey himself, as well as additional pioneers, including Rudolf Steiner (1861–1925) and Maria Montessori (1870–1952), all of whom agreed that education needed to focus on the inner dimensions of the growing child.

II. Transcendentalist educators were philosophical idealists whose ideas flowed out into other social reforms that could be broadly linked to education.

A. Such idealism derives from the Platonic notion that knowledge already exists in the mind, as in the story of Socrates teaching the slave-boy geometry.
   1. The Latin root word *educere* means to draw out what already lies within.
   2. This Neo-Platonic and Wordsworthian view is threatening to traditional ideas because, by granting wisdom to children, it reverses the normal structures of

authority: adult over child, clergy over laity, institution over individual. This shift would lead such liberal educators as Alcott into trouble with the public.

3. Elizabeth Peabody argued that children's educational levels should be linked to their emerging innate abilities, emphasizing a Platonic, Kantian, and Transcendentalist belief in intuitive knowledge.

4. Approached from this point of view, education was a matter of drawing out, not imposing ideas on the young.

5. For Alcott, Peabody, Thoreau, and even Emerson, education was not about accumulating facts; it was about the moral and spiritual development of a complete person throughout an entire life.

6. Discussion and interactive conversation were always central to this process.

B. In addition to Pestalozzi, educational theorists who contributed to these ways of thinking included Joseph Marie de Gerando, along with Richard Lovell and Maria Edgeworth, the English father and daughter.

1. Elizabeth Peabody published *First Lessons in Grammar on the Plan of Pestalozzi* and jointly translated de Gerando's *Self-Education; or, The Means and Art of Moral Progress* with Dr. Channing; both books appeared anonymously in 1830.

2. Thoreau, Fuller, Emerson, Alcott, and Ripley were all directly influenced by aspects of the Frenchman de Gerando's work in the history of philosophy and educational theory.

3. The Edgeworths' *Practical Education* (1798) advocated learning through play and what we would now call the discovery method.

4. Such progressive ideas could lead to problems, as when Alcott, in 1836–1837, published two volumes of *Conversations with Children on the Gospels* under his own name. The work included skeptical questions about religion, as well as frank discussions of human anatomy and the physical details of birth.

5. Although tame to us now, Alcott's version of religious inquiry, and of the birds-and-bees, was described by a critic at the time as "one-third absurd, one-third

blasphemous, and one-third obscene." Such free thought challenged public morality and the authority of the church and family.

6. Emerson hurried to defend Alcott in the press, but public outcry against this work and such actions as enrolling a black child in the Temple School caused the student body to shrink to the point where the school had to close.

C. In addition to specific education reforms, another important legacy of these thinkers was the idea that the human mind is constantly engaged in the process of learning, from birth until death.

1. Thoreau and Emerson, among others, claimed that they remained open to new ideas throughout adult life. As Emerson puts it in "The American Scholar," "Is not, indeed, every man a student […]?"

2. The larger implication of this way of thinking was the view that a person's understanding of the world might change and, along with it, one's beliefs and allegiances; this presents a dynamic, rather than a static, model of learning and its impact.

3. Adult education and continuing education emerge directly from this idea.

III. Margaret Fuller, Elizabeth Peabody, and Bronson Alcott all contributed to another new and Transcendentalist form of education, the collective conversation.

A. The idea of children or adults gathered in a circle in conversation with an enthusiastic teacher has become a mainstay of modern education.

1. Such a model clearly emphasizes process over product; the interaction among the minds of the learners is seen as superior to any ideology, data, dogma, or doctrine.

2. We owe to those idealistic Transcendentalists the roots of our own ideas about a wide range of educational ideas: kindergarten, less formal classes, mandatory public schools, adult book groups, and lifelong learning.

3. Now, of course, cognitive researchers and doctors tell us that the best way to keep the mind healthy is to keep it active throughout adult life.

B. It therefore goes without saying that The Teaching Company's Great Courses embody a series of ideas about education that trace their origins directly to the New England Transcendentalists.

  1. Education should be available to all—the more widely accessible and distributed, the better.

  2. The classic works of all cultures remain significant in all eras.

  3. The more we learn, the more we see important connections between and among ideas.

Essential Reading:

Vásquez, Mark G. *Authority and Reform: Religious and Educational Discourses in Nineteenth-Century New England Literature.*

Tozer, Steven E., Paul C. Violas, and Guy B. Senese. *School and Society: Historical and Contemporary Perspectives.*

Supplementary Reading:

Rosa, Alfred F. "Alcott and Montessori."

Questions to Consider:

1. What were the obvious connections between the thoughts of early Transcendentalists and educational theory?

2. Do you see strains of Transcendentalist thinking still evident in our current ideas about the education of the young?

Lecture Eighteen—Transcript
Transcendentalism and Education

Hello again. As we have already seen in some detail, the link between Transcendentalism and education was a close one. As one scholar has noted, all of the major Transcendentalists—Emerson, Thoreau, Fuller, Palmer, Alcott, Brownson, Very and more—spent years in the classroom as teachers and all had found traditional education to be inadequate and stultifying.

A number of the leading Transcendentalists were teachers or educators either briefly or for most of their careers. Others, such as Emerson, had a direct and continuing influence on a number of important educational reformers. Indeed, the very notion of education not only for children, but for all the mass of undereducated Americans in the 19th century was at the heart of one strain of Transcendentalism. We need to remember that education during this time was not simply a function of public or private schools, but also took place in the pulpit, the public lecture hall, the experimental community and certainly on the part of private tutors such as Thoreau. Indeed, the transmission of ideas from one mind to another, or from one mind to a group of minds, was at the center of a whole range of revolutionary ideals—from Brook Farm to Alcott's Temple School and even down to current ideas about the need for ongoing educational reform and lifelong learning.

Education was central to the Transcendentalist for numerous reasons. At its most basic level, education has always fundamentally been about the way ideas came into or perhaps remained active within the mind. In fact, there are a series of debates that have gone on throughout western history about the nature of knowledge that relate closely to ideas about education. Let me go through some of those by way of introduction.

The first question is whether the mind is passive, like a mirror on reality, what is called the mimetic theory, the idea that the mind simply reflects the images of reality as a mirror reflects that which stands in front of it. This idea, that the mind was passive, is the idea that in a sense dominated educational theory for most of western history.

The alternative is the possibility that the mind is active and this, as we should already sense, is a very Romantic idea, the idea of an organic mind, a mind that is part of the actual process of understanding. That should be a phrase that is memorable to us since that is the idea that Immanuel Kant had argued for; that the kind of knowledge he was interested in was the knowledge of the mind engaged in the activity of helping to create what constituted reality.

For all of the Transcendentalists, minds had to be the active creators of their own experience. That is to say the mind is not simply a passive receptor of objective or material data from outside, which it then processes. The mind, based on its own activity, helps to contribute to the way knowledge becomes developed within each individual. This idea, I think we might say, contributes to what we could call a democracy of thought. There is that word, "democracy" again, but applied once more to an intellectual concept, a democracy of thought in which each person was a potential creative artist, a creator of the ideas in his or her own mind or a potential reformer of society.

In this sense, education has always been a social issue linked directly to the organization of groups of human beings into different versions of society. Sometimes education was imagined taking place primarily in the home; in other contexts, going back once again as far as the Greeks, education was seen as the province of the state. The larger question surrounding these ideas in the 19th century included asking who was entitled to receive an education and who decided who was so entitled. Those kinds of questions, of course, had important class implications. Was education only going to be the province of the aristocracy and the upper classes or should every member of society be entitled to some version of education or the same version? Was education going to be conducted as a public or as a private phenomenon? That is to say was it the responsibility of the state to finance education or did education only occur when private resources could be marshaled to benefit certain groups of individuals? And of course, as we know, was education to be church supported or state supported? Education had long been the province of certain religious denominations and there had been associations between theological ideas and certain kinds of schools that went back as far as the Middle Ages. By the 19th century, with increasing pressure for more widespread public education, that whole question of the relationship between church and state in education became even more intense.

Who provided the education and what qualifications might be required for the teachers in individual school settings? Even those were questions that had not been resolved by the time people such as Emerson and his followers were starting to think about these ideas.

Finally, was the purpose of education to be liberal? What we would think of as the liberal arts and the classical ideal of that sort of learning? Or was education meant to be practical, designed to give people real means of making a living? Or was education supposed to be both?

We should remind ourselves that even in Europe, and certainly in America, the idea of general public education for all of the masses was still a brand new idea in the middle of the 19th century. It was only after the Transcendentalists in the last three decades, even two decades, of the 19th century that public education became a generally accepted ideal.

It is worth noting that all transcendental ideas about education were what we would have to call progressive. You will remember that Emerson and Thoreau, like their friends Alcott and Elizabeth Peabody, all gave credit to young people for the value of their own innocence, for their intuitive insights which were argued in some sense to arrive with each individual at birth and also for what we would have to see as the inherent wisdom of children. We will also remember that each of those ideas almost reversed the traditional view of children as not having special characteristics.

A key source for Transcendentalist ideas about education was a name that we have heard a couple of times in earlier lectures; that was the Swiss humanitarian and educator, Johann Pestalozzi. He was born in 1746 and he followed Rousseau in the belief in what was seen as the "inner dignity" of each child, the notion that the child, in a sense, possessed characteristics and aspects that had to be recognized and valued by the educator.

Important educators, subsequently influenced by the Transcendentalists, included Francis Parker who developed the idea of primary schools and the PTA—the Parent Teacher Association—and whom the 20th-century educator, John Dewey, called the "father of progressive education." Of course, Dewey himself, as well as additional pioneers such as Rudolf Steiner and Maria Montessori—all of these educational leaders who were born in the 19th century, but whose views continued into the 20th century—agreed that certain aspects of education had to focus on these inner dimensions, these innate aspects of the growing child.

Transcendentalist educators, as we can piece together by now, were almost always philosophical idealists, whose ideas flowed out into other social reforms that could be broadly linked to education, not just the question of what happens in formal school classrooms, as we will see. This kind of philosophical idealism, you will remember, derives from Plato's idea that knowledge, in some sense, already exists in the mind of the young child and it needs only to be extracted by the teacher. Socrates gives a famous example where he takes an uneducated slave boy and Socrates draws a series of geometric diagrams into the sand and the young boy, without any formal education, is able to draw all sorts of conclusions, simply based on the questions that Socrates asks. It is the famous example that proves, according to Plato, that ideas already exist in the mind and only need to be drawn out by a series of well argued questions.

The Latin root word from which we derive education, *educere*, means to draw out, that is to say to draw out ideas that already lie within. And this Neo-Platonic view or this Platonic view brought into the 19th century is also very close to the ideas of a Romantic poet such as Wordsworth. It is an idea that is very threatening to traditional ideas about education because it grants wisdom to the child, and by doing so, it reverses the normal structures of authority. The normal structure places the adult over the child, the clergy over the laity and the institution over the individual. In the case of this idealistic view, it is the individual, the laity or the childlike aspect of each individual that knows something that only needs to be released. This shift would lead a number of these liberal 19th-century educators such as Bronson Alcott into some trouble with the public, as we have already noted.

Elizabeth Peabody, in line with this way of thinking, argued that each child's educational level should be linked to their emerging innate abilities. That is to say, the idea that there are certain kinds of learning, certain kinds of questioning appropriate for each child at each stage of development. Indeed, this idea emphasizes precisely the Platonic, Kantian and Transcendentalist belief I have been describing in the value of intuitive knowledge.

If we approach education from this point of view, you can see by now that education becomes a matter of drawing out, not of imposing ideas on the mind of the young person. We are not simply cramming prepackaged information into the head of a child; we are placing the child in a situation where his or her innate awareness and abilities can blossom.

For Alcott, Peabody, Thoreau and even Emerson, education was thus not about accumulating facts; it was about what we would have to call the moral and spiritual development of a complete person, not only in childhood, not only in adolescence, but throughout an entire life. This is a process that continues from the moment that we are born until the end of our life.

It should also be obvious by now that activities such as discussion and interactive conversation were always central to this process. It was not just a question of listening to the teacher impose ideas from without, it was a matter of engaging the student in forms of dialog. In addition to thinkers such as Pestalozzi, educational theorists who contributed to these ideas included a number of individuals—Joseph Marie de Gerando, Richard Lovell and Maria Edgeworth, the English father and daughter combination.

Elizabeth Peabody herself published *First Lessons in Grammar on the Plan of Pestalozzi* and then she jointly translated de Gerando's *Self-Education, or, The Means and Art of Moral Progress*; she translated that work with Dr. Channing. Both of these books appeared anonymously in 1830. That "anonymous" is interesting because I think it suggests partly that these ideas were too controversial to be attached to the names of the publishers and translators.

Thoreau, Fuller, Emerson, Alcott and Ripley were all directly influenced by aspects of the Frenchman's—de Gerando's—work on the history of philosophy and educational theory. In much the same way that I have been trying to do in the introduction to this lecture, de Gerando connected the history of philosophy itself with these emerging ideas about the best way to educate individuals.

The Edgeworths, father and daughter, published *Practical Education* in 1798 in which they advocated learning through play—I think what we would now call the discovery method—the idea that experiential forms of learning could also benefit the growing mind of the child.

As we have already seen, such progressive ideas as these might lead to problems, as with Alcott in 1836 and 1837, when he published two volumes of his *Conversations with Children on the Gospels* and signed that book with his own name. This work, as you may remember, included a series of skeptical questions about religion that required answers from the children as well as frank discussions about human anatomy and the physical details of birth. Of course, Alcott might have been thinking that there were certain levels of knowledge that were appropriate for children at certain ages, even if his scale did not agree with Peabody's or someone else's.

Although really quite tame to us now, Alcott's version of this religious-based inquiry, and especially of the birds and the bees, was described by one critic at the time as "One-third absurd, one-third blasphemous, and one-third obscene." Such freedom of thought, however, challenged public morality in ways that will be obvious and also challenged the authority of the church and the family. I think that the other important point to note here is that educational ideas, especially when they came from outside, especially when they were imposed by teachers or especially by the state, could easily come into conflict with family values or principles of how children should be educated and into conflict with religious principles. We still see versions of that debate around us in our own time.

Once Alcott was in trouble for the publication of these unacceptable ideas, Emerson hurried to defend him in the public press. But outcry against Alcott's work and the fact that that publication was almost immediately followed by Alcott enrolling an African-American child at the Temple School caused the student body of his school to shrink to the point where it had to close. Therefore, I do not want us to think that any set of ideas about education would be allowed to flourish in the climate of the middle of the 19th century.

In addition to specific educational reforms, another important legacy of all of these thinkers was the idea that the human mind is constantly engaged in the process of learning. If the mind in this romantic model, that traces back at least to Rousseau, is an active agent, constantly engaged in the process of its own development—

and remember that romantic ideal traces not just to Rousseau, but as far back as Plato—that a mind obviously never stops functioning. It continues to learn and to develop throughout a lifetime.

Thoreau and Emerson, among others, claimed that they remained open to all sorts of new ideas and to all sorts of new learning throughout their adult life. Clearly one of the principles of any individual who maintains a journal throughout a lifetime, as many of these figures did, is the idea that every day becomes an opportunity for the reading of a new book, the discovery of a new idea or the exposure to a new individual that changes a person's way of thinking.

Emerson puts this very succinctly in his essay, "The American Scholar." He said "Is not, indeed, every man a student." I think the emphasis there on the adult version of "man" is very important. Emerson wants to remind us that each of us—of course we would say male or female—remains a student at whatever point in life we find ourselves. The larger implication of this idea is the view that a person's understanding of the world might change, and along with that, the idea that one's beliefs and even allegiances might alter. This presents what we would have to describe as a dynamic, not a static, model of learning and especially of the impact of education. I think this notion of dynamism in education also helps us to understand precisely the sorts of religious questioning that we have seen throughout the series of lectures—only a person who was open to new ways of thinking would ever be able to challenge either the ideology of their ancestors or the specific beliefs they had inherited from parents or from earlier cultural ways of imagining the world. Therefore, the principle that each time we learn something, we are in a position to change our way of thinking, also seems to relate directly to these more progressive ideas about education.

As Emerson and Thoreau would almost have it—I am in a position in any particular moment in my life where I could learn a new fact, be exposed to a new idea or even see something I had already known in a slightly different way, and at that moment, my way of understanding things could suddenly change.

In this sense, adult education and what we now think of as continuing education, not stopping with the end of high school, not ending when we conclude our formal university training, but the idea of education as a process that extends through life, is clearly tied to these Transcendentalist ideas. In this sense Margaret Fuller, Elizabeth Peabody, Bronson Alcott and others all contributed to this new and Transcendentalist form of education, which came to be known as the collective conversation. It is with that idea that I would like to conclude.

The idea of children, or especially of adults, gathered in a circle, in conversation with an enthusiastic teacher has become a mainstay of modern education. Even as simple a principle as changing the organization of a classroom from the traditional model of students ranging in desks in rows and lines, with a teacher or a professor at the front of a classroom, to a circular arrangement in which the teacher becomes one participant in a circular conversation suggests just this sort of change toward a conversational or a discussion-based model of education. This model clearly emphasizes the process of education over the product; that is to say, something happens while people are engaged in a conversation that would not happen otherwise because each of the minds has to be engaged in what is going on. In that sense, the interaction among the minds of the learners is seen as superior to any specific ideology, any particular batch of data, any formal external dogma or certainly any doctrine. Once again, we see the way that principles of education can actually leads to certain kinds of questions that would not be able to be asked under other models of educational organization.

We owe, I think, to those idealistic Transcendentalists the roots of our own ideas about a whole range of educational ideas. I hope by now, this list will be clear—kindergarten comes out of their appreciation of the value of young minds and of the importance of grabbing those minds while they are young and starting to help the process of their growth. Less formal classes suggest the right of students to engage in experiential forms of learning, where they actually participate in an activity, where they actually engage physically in doing something and learn, as we would now say, through the process of doing. Mandatory public schools emerge out of the idea that education should not simply be restricted to people who can afford to pay for certain kinds of education, should not just be restricted to the aristocracy or to certain members of certain classes; it should be a guaranteed right of all individuals. Of course the idea of adult book groups is very closely connected to something like the Elizabeth Peabody or Margaret Fuller "Conversation," where a group of adults gather, chooses a reading and then decides to discuss that reading in terms of each person's bringing his or her own contribution to the debate, and as I have suggested, the question of lifelong learning, the fact that learning does not stop when the classroom door closes.

Now it is even the case that cognitive researchers are telling us that the best way to keep an individual human mind healthy is to keep it active throughout adult life. We often have heard that the Greek teachers would walk back and forth; in the famous example of Aristotle's school, the teacher and the students would walk back and forth together and for that reason, the school came to be known as the Peripatetics.

It now turns out, according to one of my colleagues who is a cognitive researcher, that the actual process of physically moving around while in the process of teaching results in more oxygen to the brain and as a result, both the students and the teachers may benefit from some physical activity associated with the engagement with ideas. In a similar way, we now know that one of the best ways to keep the mind young is to keep it active throughout life.

It should, by now, go without saying that The Teaching Company's *Great Courses* embody a set of ideas about education that, I would argue, trace their origins directly back to those New England Transcendentalists. Education should be available to all, the more widely accessible and the more widely distributed the better.

The classic works of all cultures remain significant in all eras and will remain significant for all time. The more we learn, the more we see important connections between and among the most important ideas.

With that, let us turn to the question of social activism, especially in one of its most extreme Transcendentalist versions.

Lecture Nineteen
Thoreau, Abolition, and John Brown

Scope:

From education, we move to the question of social activism. The trial and execution of John Brown after his slave revolt and raid on the armory at Harpers Ferry, Virginia (now West Virginia), produced extensive commentary and debate in abolitionist and Transcendentalist circles. John Brown was at once celebrated as a divinely inspired individual and reviled as a bloodthirsty lunatic. Thoreau, who had met Brown long before the raid, weighed in as a supporter of Brown's ideals, if not his actions, even though this view seemed to complicate Thoreau's earlier ideas about civil disobedience. Brown's actions were important not only because they galvanized issues that had been lurking just below the surface of American thought and political action, but also because they brought to light central questions about violent versus nonviolent action, the power of the individual, and the historical reality of change that might not always occur gradually. Numerous historians have suggested that Brown's actions and the powerful responses they provoked, such as Thoreau's, helped to hasten the onset of the American Civil War.

Outline

I. John Brown's (1800–1859) raid on Harpers Ferry was one of the most galvanizing public events in the years leading up to the Civil War. Brown's early life helps to explain why.

    A. Brown's hatred of slavery began very early and increased steadily into adulthood.

        1. His father and extended family were profoundly religious and committed abolitionists. They moved from his Connecticut birthplace to a powerfully free-state area of northern Ohio when John was still a boy.

        2. His education was cut short by eye problems, and he went on to a variety of unsuccessful careers: farmer, land speculator, wool dealer, hide tanner.

        3. He engaged in many peaceful abolitionist activities as a younger man.

4. Even in strained financial circumstances, Brown fathered 20 children by two wives, and he gave land to fugitive slaves. He and his second wife agreed to raise a black child as one of their own.

5. He contributed to the formation of the League of Gileadites, an organization that protected escaped slaves.

6. By 1849, Brown was living in a philanthropic black community in the isolated Adirondack Mountain region of New York. He offered to serve as a father figure to freed blacks and establish his own family there.

B. The mood changed, however, when Brown moved to Kansas in the 1850s.

1. By this time, he was a virulent abolitionist, and his career turned violent after following a number of his sons to the Kansas territory.

2. Once there, he led a group of antislavery guerillas in repelling a proslavery assault on the town of Lawrence.

3. A year later, in May of 1856, seeking direct revenge for another attack, Brown and half a dozen followers, including four of his own sons, dragged five unarmed people from their homes and hacked them to death.

4. More than 50 people were killed in "Bleeding Kansas" between 1854 and 1856.

II. The Harpers Ferry raid was the culmination of Brown's violent activism.

A. In his public defense, he would say he never intended violence or insurrection, but it is clear that the attack was designed to incite a full-scale slave revolt.

1. On October 16, 1859, Brown led 21 black and white men on a raid of the federal arsenal at the junction of the Potomac and Shenandoah rivers.

2. After deaths on both sides, he was stopped by local farmers, militiamen, and regular soldiers led by Robert E. Lee.

3. Both John Wilkes Booth and J. E. B. Stuart served with this military force; two of Brown's own sons were killed during the raid.

4. Brown was tried for treason in nearby Charles Town, found guilty, and hanged on December 2, 1859; on his

execution day, he wrote, with his characteristically non-grammatical punctuation, "I John Brown am now quite certain that the crimes of this guilty, land: will never be purged away; but with Blood."

B. The immediate reaction of most Americans was to see Brown as a lunatic or a fanatic, but many northern abolitionists, including some in Concord, Massachusetts, came to see him as almost a saint or, at least, as a martyr to the cause.

1. Lucretia Mott in 1860 said, "[…] it is not John Brown the soldier that we praise; it is John Brown the moral hero; John Brown the noble confessor and martyr whom we honor."

2. By the time of the Civil War, thousands of Union soldiers were singing his anthem: "John Brown's body lies a-mouldering in the grave,/But his truth is marching on."

3. More recently, historian David S. Reynolds has said that John Brown, although a "terrorist," was also a liberator who "Killed Slavery, Sparked the Civil War, and Seeded Civil Rights," quoting the subtitle of his 2005 book.

III. Countless responses to the raid and its aftermath were impassioned, nationwide, and long-lasting in their effects.

A. William Lloyd Garrison described Brown's attack as "well-intended but sadly misguided" and "wild and futile" in an article entitled "The Tragedy at Harper's Ferry" in the abolitionist newspaper *The Liberator*.

1. Although an advocate of nonviolence, Garrison defended Brown from journalistic attacks in the North and South. He claimed that American revolutionaries who had taken up arms against the unjust laws of Britain might be compared to the violent agitation of Brown, at least in principle.

2. The link between Brown and Transcendentalism is obvious. Brown implicitly and in his writings and speeches appealed to a higher law than the law of the state.

3. To some, belief in the then-illegal right of a slave to be free was a perfect example of what Thoreau and Emerson meant by a "transcendent" truth.

B. The Concord circle of Transcendentalists had known Brown well since 1857.

   1. Thoreau, among others, first met Brown when he traveled to the East Coast to raise money for what he called his "Holy War."

   2. Brown had a meal with Thoreau at the family boarding house, and the two talked at length.

   3. Brown delivered a rousing abolitionist lecture to citizens gathered in Concord Town Hall. Of the 100 in attendance, Emerson donated $25 and Thoreau, in his own words, "submitted a trifle."

C. As news of the Harpers Ferry raid and Brown's execution six weeks later spread, the zealot was remembered by most of the citizens of Concord.

   1. Thoreau, at a memorial service for Brown, delivered a eulogy in which he claimed that Brown had "a spark of divinity in him" and was "a transcendentalist above all."

   2. Shortly after the Harpers Ferry attack, Theodore Parker wrote, "One held against his will as a slave has a natural right to kill everyone who seeks to prevent his enjoyment of liberty," a view shared by many northerners.

   3. Bronson Alcott could even claim that Brown was "worthy of the glories of the cross."

   4. Thoreau summed up by saying that Brown "did not recognize unjust human laws, but resisted them as he was bid."

   5. Of course, not everyone in Concord agreed. Thoreau's friend Minott Pratt wrote that Henry David was "a little extravagant" in his praise.

   6. Edward Emerson's (son of Ralph Waldo) journal recorded that numerous Concord residents scoffed at Thoreau's "Plea for Captain John Brown."

D. This split in local and national sentiment was dramatized by the fact that while Thoreau and Alcott were singing Brown's praises inside First Parish Church, Brown was being hanged and burned in effigy by their neighbors.

1. Of course, political violence and bloodshed almost always produce powerfully opposed feelings on either side of an issue.
2. Brown's words about national bloodshed, however, were prophetic; the Civil War began in less than a year and a half, and many have said it was hastened by Brown's violent actions and death.
3. Some historians have seen him as a madman, but Union soldiers by the thousands sang his anthem as they marched to their own deaths.
4. Thoreau's words still tell us something significant: "No man in America has ever stood up so persistently and effectively for the dignity of human nature." John Brown, he concluded, was "the most American of us all."
5. To make such a claim about a man who was a thief and murderer is to begin a conversation that continues today about resistance to unjust laws, preemptive armed conflict, and even the death penalty.

Essential Reading:

Peterson, Merrill D. *John Brown: The Legend Revisited.*

Reynolds, David. *John Brown, Abolitionist: The Man Who Killed Slavery, Sparked the Civil War, and Seeded Civil Rights.*

Supplementary Reading:

Goodwin, James. "Thoreau and John Brown: Transcendental Politics."

Questions to Consider:

1. Why would an apparent pacifist such as Thoreau support the cause and actions of John Brown?
2. Do you think John Brown was insane? If so, why has he assumed such a central role in American historical memory? If not, why have so many people doubted his sanity?

Lecture Nineteen—Transcript
Thoreau, Abolition, and John Brown

From education, we now move to what we might see as the question of the extreme of social activism. The trial and execution of John Brown, after his slave revolt and raid on the armory at Harpers Ferry, Virginia—which is now part of West Virginia—produced extensive commentary and debate in a range of abolitionist and Transcendentalist circles. John Brown was at once celebrated as a divinely inspired individual and was reviled as a blood-thirsty lunatic, depending on the commentator's point of view.

Henry David Thoreau, who had actually met John Brown long before the raid, weighed in as a supporter of Brown's ideals, if not necessarily all of his actions—even though this view seems to complicate Thoreau's earlier ideas about civil disobedience in ways that we will discuss. Brown's actions were important for the time, not only because they galvanized a whole series of issues that had been lurking just below the surface of American thought and political action in the years leading up to the Civil War, but because they brought to light central questions about violent versus nonviolent actions, about the power of the individual and about the historical reality of change that might not always wait to occur in a gradual or peaceful way.

Many historians at the time, and since, have argued that Brown's actions, and powerful response, such as those of Thoreau to Brown's raid, actually helped to hasten the onset of the American Civil War. John Brown's raid on Harpers Ferry was one of the most galvanizing public events in the years leading up to the Civil War. Brown's early life, I think, helps to explain why. His own hatred of slavery began very early in his life and seems to have increased steadily until his adulthood when, in a sense, it broke out in its most extreme form. Brown's father and most of the members of his extended family were profoundly religious individuals and they were committed abolitionists. They moved from Brown's Connecticut birthplace to a powerfully free-state area of northern Ohio while John was still a boy. We need to remember that in these decades of American history, there were parts of America where slavery was still a contested question and one's affiliation with a particular region might help to identify one's attitude toward the increasingly troubling question of slavery.

Brown's formal education was cut short by eye problems—you may remember that Emerson had similar problems that restricted some of his educational potential throughout his early life—and Brown went on to a variety of unsuccessful careers, which seemed to increase his general level of frustration. He failed as a farmer, then as a land speculator, as a dealer in wool and finally as a hide tanner. Unlike a figure such as Thoreau, who seemed to have more or less success in a range of occupations, John Brown was a figure who, whatever he tried to accomplish, in a sense, seemed to fail at.

He engaged in a number of peaceful abolitionist activities as a younger man. He attended lectures, he spoke out, and there were all sorts of ways that, as the Abolitionist Movement grew in America during these decades, individuals could stake their claims on one side or the other of this question.

Even in the very strained financial circumstances that resulted from his unsuccessful careers, Brown fathered 20 children by two different wives and actually ended up giving land that he owned to a number of fugitive slaves. Eventually he and his second wife agreed to raise a black child as one of their own children, so it was clear that Brown was declaring his abolitionist views in his actions as well as in his ideas.

He contributed to the formation of an organization called the League of Gileadites, from the biblical image of the land of Gilead. This was an organization that protected escaped slaves and, as the biblical reference would suggest, tried to offer a place in which former slaves, escaped slaves, could lead a life that would be free from fear of recapture.

By 1849, Brown was living in a philanthropic black community in the isolated Adirondack Mountains region of New York. This was a community that was set up by abolitionists in order to provide one of these places where black individuals could live in relative safety with the support of white abolitionists as well. Brown offered to serve as a father figure to freed blacks, and he actually established his own family there. If you go to the Adirondack Mountains in New York today, you can actually visit a part of this farm. It, interestingly, is located right on the edge of what is now Olympic Village in Lake Placid.

This generally benevolent mood changed however, when Brown up and moved to Kansas in the 1850s. By this time, and for reasons that I think are still not completely clear to historians or his biographers, he had become increasingly virulent in his ideas about abolition and his belief that slavery needed to end throughout all of the United States. Indeed, as many of us know, his career turned violent after following a number of his own sons to the Kansas territory, a part of America that became notorious and infamous around just this question.

Once in Kansas, Brown led a group of antislavery guerillas—that is probably the best word to describe them—in repelling a proslavery assault on the town of Lawrence, Kansas, where the University of Kansas is now located. These were guerilla fighters of a kind that were willing to take up arms and use violence to bring about their aims.

A year later, in May 1856, Brown was seeking direct revenge for another attack, and he and a half dozen of his followers, including four of his own sons, dragged five unarmed people from their homes and hacked them to death. Clearly by this time, Brown's abolitionist tendencies extended to the point where anyone involved in proslavery causes or in the continuation of the institution of slavery, was seen by Brown as an absolute enemy.

He was not the only person engaged in these kinds of activities; over 50 people were killed in what came to be known as "Bleeding Kansas," between the two years, 1854 and 1856. As many historians have argued subsequently, those two years in Kansas really predicted the kind of energy and the kind of letting of blood that, in a sense, became the national crisis of the next two decades.

The raid on Harpers Ferry was without doubt, the culmination of Brown's activism and especially of his violent activism. In his public defense, after he was arrested Brown would actually say that he never intended violence or insurrection, but these remarks have to be put in context of the fact that his attack on the armory was clearly designed to incite a full-scale slave revolt. The people who actually engaged in the raid included both blacks and whites, and it is obvious that the sole purpose for attacking this cache of arms was to gain more weapons to extend the slave revolt further into the state of Virginia.

Here is what actually happened. On October 16, 1859, Brown led twenty-one black and white men on a raid of the federal arsenal at the junction of the Potomac and the Shenandoah Rivers. At this point, the town of Harpers Ferry was still in the state of Virginia. As many of you will know, after the Civil War, West Virginia was separated, as a separate state on its own. That is why the town is now considered part of West Virginia.

After deaths on both sides of this engagement, Brown and his attackers were stopped by a group of local farmers, militia men and eventually—and somewhat ironically I suppose—by a group of regular soldiers led by, of all people, Robert E. Lee. Robert E. Lee was still serving in the Union Army in 1859, and he was sent out with this group of armed soldiers to quell this violent uprising.

It is also worth noting that both John Wilkes Booth and J. E. B. Stuart served with this military force. Here we have a remarkable conjunction of John Brown, Robert E. Lee, John Wilkes Booth and J. E. B. Stuart, all in this tiny town where the Potomac and the Shenandoah Rivers meet. It is also the case that two of Brown's own sons were killed during this raid, so by this point it was clear that Brown was willing to sacrifice almost everything in his efforts to bring about an end to slavery.

Brown was captured and was tried for treason in nearby Charles Town. He was found guilty and was hanged on December 2, 1859. On his execution day he wrote, with his own characteristically non-grammatical punctuation and diction, a phrase that has echoed from that day until this, "I John Brown am now quite certain that the crimes of this guilty, land: will never be purged away, but with Blood." Whatever John Brown's state of mind at the time of the raid on Harpers Ferry, it is clear that he had a very prophetic sense of the mood in America and of the conditions that were likely to unfold before many years had passed.

The immediate reaction on the part of most Americans, as we might expect, was to see Brown as either a lunatic or a fanatic, at least a fanatic. But interestingly, many Northern abolitionists, including a number of our Transcendentalist friends, in and around Concord, Massachusetts, actually came to see him as almost a saint, or at least a martyr to the cause of abolition. Here is what Lucretia Mott said in 1860, "[...] it is not John Brown the soldier that we praise; it is John

Brown the moral hero; John Brown the noble confessor and martyr whom we honor."

In Mott's interesting construction we see the distinction between Brown as a soldier, whom we will hold off from praising, and Brown as a moral hero or martyr to a higher cause. Once I use that phrase "higher cause," I think we start to have a sense of how the Transcendentalist way of thinking might enter into this historical event.

By the time of the Civil War, we probably need to remember that thousands of Union Soldiers were singing his anthem, "John Brown's body lies a-mouldering in the grave,/But his truth is marching on." Therefore, the support for Brown that may have seemed extreme or unusual in certain liberal New England circles in 1859 and 1860, was certainly much more widespread by the time of the Civil War itself. Indeed, if we bring this question forward to our own times, most recently in a 2005 book, historian, David S. Reynolds, has said that John Brown on the one hand was a "terrorist," but he is also rightly seen as a liberator who "Killed Slavery, Sparked the Civil War and Seeded Civil Rights." Here in a biography of 2005, Reynolds is willing to link the tension of describing Brown as a terrorist with also seeing him as someone who ended slavery, sparked the Civil War and also had connections to the Civil Rights Movement in our own era.

Countless responses to Brown's raid and its immediate aftermath were impassioned, nationwide and, as I have just suggested, clearly long lasting in their effects. William Lloyd Garrison, the famous, although peaceful, abolitionist described Brown's attack as "well intended but sadly misguided." I suspect that was closer to what we would think of as the general view; people could understand the motivation behind Brown's actions, but Garrison wanted to call them misguided. Garrison also referred to them as "wild and futile," suggesting a kind of extremity and also a sense in which they had not succeeded in their initial efforts.

Garrison published these views in an article entitled "The Tragedy at Harpers Ferry," in the widely read Abolitionist newspaper, *The Liberator*. Although Garrison was an advocate of nonviolence throughout his career as an abolitionist, he defended Brown from a number of more intense and extreme journalistic attacks in the North and the South. Garrison argued that American revolutionaries who had been forced to take up arms against the unjust laws of Britain might be compared to the violent agitations of Brown, at least in principle. Once again, when I refer to "taking up arms against an unjust law," we may start to see a link to a Transcendentalist principle we will remember from an earlier lecture.

By this time, the link between Brown and Transcendentalism, I hope, will start to become obvious. Brown implicitly, not only in his actions at Harpers Ferry, but also in his writings and a number of his abolitionist speeches, appealed to a higher law than the law of the State. To some people, belief in the then-illegal right of a slave to be free, in the South, was a perfect example of what Thoreau and Emerson meant by a "transcendent" truth. That is to say, there were principles that were higher than the laws of the State, and when a person, through their innate moral sense, intuited this sense of a truth that was higher than the truth of the law, they had an implicit, not only right, but responsibility, Thoreau argued in "Civil Disobedience," to break that law.

The Concord circle of Transcendentalists had known John Brown well since 1857, two years before the raid. Thoreau, among others, had first met John Brown when he traveled up the East Coast to raise money for what he called his "Holy War." Brown, in fact, actually had a meal with Thoreau at the Thoreau family boarding house and the two talked at length at a time when Brown was still seen as a peaceful abolitionist and certainly had nothing of the reputation that he would eventually gain.

At this same time, Brown delivered a rousing abolitionist lecture to a group of citizens who were gathered at the Concord Town Hall. Of the hundred or so, people in attendance, it is worth noting perhaps that Emerson donated $25 to Brown's cause and Thoreau, in his own words, "submitted a trifle."

Now if we jump forward to the aftermath of the Harpers Ferry raid, as news of Harpers Ferry and of Brown's execution six weeks later spread rapidly through America, this figure of such a strong zealot was remembered by many of those citizens who had met him two years earlier in Concord. Thoreau attended a memorial service for Brown—memorial services were held all the way up the northern states of America among abolitionist circles—Thoreau attended one of these memorial services and, indeed, delivered a eulogy in which he claimed that Brown had "a spark of divinity in him" and most interesting for our purposes, Thoreau said that Brown was "a Transcendentalist above all." Now the link is stated in Thoreau's own words. Whatever Brown's actions, his willingness to serve a higher principle than the law of the land links him with a set of ideas that Thoreau wants to describe as Transcendental.

Shortly after the Harpers Ferry attack, Theodore Parker wrote, "One held against his will as a slave has a natural right to kill everyone who seeks to prevent his enjoyment of liberty." This became a view shared by many Northerners. Although of course, as we saw in our lecture about Parker, this willingness to see a slave's right to kill his master or anyone who seeks to "prevent his liberty," as Parker said, was also seen as an extreme position that many more moderate people found they had a hard time accepting.

Bronson Alcott, perhaps not surprisingly, could even go so far as to claim that Brown was "worthy of the glories of the cross," almost identifying Brown as a Christ-like figure who was willing to sacrifice his own life for a higher truth.

I think Thoreau summed up this series of Transcendentalist reactions to Brown's life when he said that Brown "did not recognize unjust human laws, but resisted them as he was bid." Here again is that important distinction—do I accept an unjust human law or do I resist that law in service of a higher cause?

Of course, as I have hinted, not everyone, even in Concord, agreed with the intensity of these reactions to Brown's life and to his death. Thoreau's friend, Minott Pratt, for example, wrote that Henry David, in the eulogy he delivered, was "a little extravagant" in his praise. And Edward Emerson, who was one of the sons of Ralph Waldo, included a comment in his journal that numerous Concord residents actually scoffed, when Thoreau gave his plea for Captain John Brown.

This clear split in local and national sentiment was dramatized by the fact that while Thoreau and Alcott were singing Brown's praises inside of the First Parish Church, Brown, at the same time, was being hanged and burned in effigy right outside by their neighbors. I think what is important for our purposes, in terms of this lecture, is to recognize how Brown's life and his actions, as almost all historians have argued, forced the question. It was really the raid on Harpers

Ferry that in some sense galvanized people's thinking and forced everyone, even those who had managed to avoid stating their opinions either about slavery or about abolition, to take a stand and to stake their claim.

It is also worth noting that Thoreau, who is often mistakenly called a pacifist, as we have seen in one of our earlier lectures, Thoreau is really much more concerned with the individual's right to practice forms of civil disobedience—that is to separate himself or herself from the laws of the state—than Thoreau is interested in saying that nonviolence is always, or the only, response to certain forms of unjust laws. Once again, I think, considering the circumstances surrounding Brown's raid, let us remind ourselves not to make the mistake of associating Thoreau's ideas of civil disobedience with always passive resistance.

Having said that, it is also important to remember that in all of Thoreau's writings—unlike some of the more extremist defenders of Brown—Thoreau does want to distinguish his support of the ideas behind Brown's actions from Brown's actual methods. Clearly any social action that results in the death of one's own children or that brings about the end of one's own life, and therefore, the end of one's cause, produces a whole series of conflicting responses. On the one hand, people can say Brown was far too extreme in his actions; on the other hand, clearly it makes sense for us to understand, even today, how Brown's actions did help to precipitate the events that would lead to Fort Sumter.

The split that I have been describing in national and local sentiment was pretty much felt throughout the country. Of course, political violence and bloodshed almost always produce powerfully opposed feelings on either side of an issue. Whenever there is violence brought about by political circumstances, or whenever people die in service of a cause, the result is almost always that people, as I have said, have to take a stand on one side or the other.

Brown's words about national bloodshed, and the fact that the problem he is trying to solve, will only be ultimately ended by the shedding of blood, were extremely prophetic. The Civil War began in less than a year and a half and many have argued that it was directly hastened by Brown's violent actions and by his death; once again, the notion that a martyr of a certain kind may bring the issue to the forefront in a way that would not have happened otherwise.

Some historians—then and now—have continued to see Brown as a madman. But, as I have argued, Union Soldiers, by the thousands, were singing his anthem, as they marched to their own deaths, within a couple of years. Thoreau's own words, I think, still tell us something very significant. Here is another of Thoreau's comments from his eulogy on Brown, "No man in America has ever stood up so persistently and effectively for the dignity of human nature." Then Thoreau concluded by saying that "John Brown was the most American of us all." To make such a claim about a man who was a thief and a murderer is to begin a continuing conversation about resistance to unjust laws, about preemptive armed conflict and perhaps even about the legitimacy of the death penalty.

From here we will move to consider another extremely significant American, Frederick Douglass.

Lecture Twenty
Frederick Douglass

Scope:

Now we will begin an examination of several figures who, although they might not have identified themselves with the label Transcendentalist, nevertheless were sufficiently influenced by, or so influential within, the movement that they deserve to be discussed in these lectures. The first such individual is Frederick Douglass: fugitive slave, abolitionist, freethinker, eventual advisor to presidents. Douglass met many leading Transcendentalist figures during the time that he lectured in Boston and Concord. More important, Douglass's life was seen as a perfect embodiment of Transcendentalist ideals. A runaway slave and leader of the Underground Railroad, he was largely self-educated yet became a bestselling author and counselor to Abraham Lincoln. He began publishing *The North Star*, a widely circulated abolitionist periodical, during the same year that the first women's rights convention was held at Seneca Falls. As a lecturer, editor, campaigner for women's rights, and political appointee, Douglass revealed that the power of one person's ideas might become the embodied truth of an entire social movement.

Outline

I. Frederick Douglass (1818–1895) was a sort of Martin Luther King, Jr., for the 19th century: public speaker, author, editor, activist, and civil-rights campaigner.

    A. Douglass's life and words have often been seen as a living example of the ideals of the New England Transcendentalists.

        1. As a runaway slave, he was virtually self-educated.

        2. His journalism and lecturing connected him to important developing media of the time, giving him a platform and a public.

        3. His life and work as an abolitionist came to stand for the moralist as an individual above all else. He broke with both William Lloyd Garrison and John Brown, for example, in favor of the power of his own vision.

4. By the time of his death at the end of the century, he had come to represent the authority of a single soul trying to bring about sweeping social change.

B. In the course of his long career, Douglass lectured in both Boston and Concord and met Emerson, Thoreau, Dr. Channing, and Theodore Parker.

    1. Emerson had spoken out in public against slavery for the first time in 1844; by 1851, he attacked the Fugitive Slave Law in front of the people of Concord: "An immoral law makes it a man's duty to break it [...] Let us respect the Union to all honest ends. But also respect an older and wider union, the law of Nature and rectitude."

    2. Emerson concluded, and many abolitionists came to agree, that the law that would lead to the recapture of runaway slaves needed to be "wiped out of the statute-book; but whilst it stands there, it must be disobeyed."

    3. Douglass initially joined these Concordians in support of John Brown; in fact, he became a confidante of Brown up until the time of the Harpers Ferry raid.

C. His great public power derived initially from the effect of his oratory.

    1. Douglass's early speeches dealt mainly with his own experiences; some refused to believe that he had been a slave.

    2. Those who heard him speak reported the dramatic power of the oratory. He described slave-owners beating slaves of every sort, a young girl's head "covered with festering sores," and the practice of breeding slaves like prized animals. Some of these details were news at the time to northerners.

    3. "I have often been awakened at the dawn of day by the most heart-rending shrieks of an own aunt of mine, whom [Mr. Plummer] used to tie up to a joist, and whip upon her naked back till she was literally covered with blood. No words, no tears, no prayers, from his gory victim, seemed to move his iron heart from its bloody purpose. The louder she screamed, the harder he whipped; and where the blood ran fastest, there he whipped longest. He would whip her to make her scream, and whip her to make her hush; and not until overcome by fatigue, would he cease to swing the blood-clotted cowskin" (*Narrative*, 1845).

4. He even used humor to good effect, as in his retelling of the moment when he "broke the slave breaker" named Edward Covey by fighting back, an-unheard-of response at the time. Likewise, he offered a laughable imitation of clergy in their pulpits promising slaves that God would be angered if they dared disobey their owners and masters.

II. From his birth into slavery until his death as an international figure, Douglass fought tirelessly for the rights of black Americans, and he linked those rights to the rights of all human beings.

A. Born a slave on the eastern shore of Maryland in 1818, he was the son of a white man and a slave woman whom he saw only several times in his life.

1. He escaped once and was recaptured, an event he recorded as one of his most terrible experiences: freedom achieved, then taken away.

2. He escaped for good when he was 20 by impersonating a sailor, but in certain places, he was still a fugitive for decades until the Civil War ended.

3. He had met the free black woman Anna Murray while he was still enslaved; they married and moved north to Massachusetts to begin a family.

B. Douglass soon lectured for the Massachusetts Anti-Slavery Society and met William Lloyd Garrison.

1. His career as a public speaker and writer flourished; who but a former slave could speak or write with this accuracy and conviction?

2. Douglass began a related career in 1847 with the first publication of *The North Star*, a weekly to rival Garrison's *Liberator*; Douglass's masthead motto was: "Right is of no sex—Truth is of no color—God is the Father of us all, and we are all Brethren."

3. In 1848 he attended the first convention for women's rights held at Seneca Falls, where he linked the struggles of slaves with the struggles of oppressed women.

4. Douglass traveled to England, where he claimed to have felt fully free for the first time and where he came to link the rights of slaves to the rights of oppressed people of all kinds. His lectures supported women, Irish home rule, and the temperance movement. He returned to England later, when he was worried about being linked to Brown's raid and execution.

C. By the time of the Civil War, Douglass was enough of a public figure to be called to the White House for meetings with Lincoln.

1. Lincoln called him "my friend Douglass."

2. Douglass's influence also helped him to become a recruiter for black soldiers, eventually totaling two companies, including two sons of Douglass.

3. He went on to meet with Andrew Johnson after the war to discuss the rights of former slaves and the complex issues surrounding Reconstruction.

D. After the end of the Civil War, Douglass actively supported the constitutional amendments that made equal rights a matter of law.

1. The issue was by no means settled, however. Douglass consistently lamented the lack of real opportunity for black people and the continuing separation of the races.

2. He claimed that racism was not merely "a southern problem."

3. After the Civil War, he wrote, "Did John Brown fail? [...] John Brown began the war that ended American slavery and made this a free Republic. [...] His zeal in the cause of my race was far greater than mine."

4. Late in life, and after the death of his first wife, Douglass married his white former secretary. He silenced critics of this marriage by saying that his mother's race was honored by his first marriage, his father's race by his second marriage.

III. The legacy of Douglass was widespread and powerful in America and beyond.

A. His writings were bestsellers, and he spoke out publicly until the end of his life.

1. *Narrative of the Life of Frederick Douglass, An American Slave* (1845) was his first book.
2. *My Bondage, My Freedom* (1855) described his first trip to England and added, "What to the Slave is the Fourth of July?":

> The blessings in which you, this day, rejoice, are not enjoyed in common. The rich inheritance of justice, liberty, prosperity and independence, bequeathed by your fathers, is shared by you, not by me. The sunlight that brought life and healing to you, has brought stripes and death to me. This Fourth [of] July is yours, not mine. You may rejoice, I must mourn. To drag a man in fetters into the grand illuminated temple of liberty, and call upon him to join you in joyous anthems, were inhuman mockery and sacrilegious irony.

3. In 1881, he published the third of his autobiographical volumes, *Life and Times of Frederick Douglass*. Each subsequent volume added more details and more candor.

B. Many, including the poet Paul Laurence Dunbar, celebrated Douglass: "To sin and crime he gave their proper hue,/And hurled at evil what was evil's due."

1. Douglass's "What to the Slave is the Fourth of July?" has been compared to Martin Luther King, Jr.'s "I Have a Dream" speech, not in terms of optimism, but rather, in recognition of, in King's words, the "withering injustice" at the heart of American democracy and a continuing "lonely island of poverty in the midst of a vast ocean of material prosperity."

2. Douglass, finally, wanted to make the grand promises of America available to all of America's citizens. The work of his legacy clearly continues.

Essential Reading:

Douglass, Frederick. *Autobiographies*: *Narrative of the Life of Frederick Douglass, An American Slave*; *My Bondage and My Freedom*; *Life and Times of Frederick Douglass*. Ed. Henry Louis Gates.

Martin, Waldo E., Jr. *The Mind of Frederick Douglass*.

Supplementary Reading:

DeLombard, Jeannine. "'Eye-Witness to the Cruelty': Southern Violence and Northern Testimony in Frederick Douglass's 1845 *Narrative*."

Questions to Consider:

1. Why was it so difficult for a black man to get his ideas taken seriously in the middle of the 19th century?

2. How was Douglass able to break down the barriers that separated him from white society and become such a powerful and influential individual?

Lecture Twenty—Transcript
Frederick Douglass

Now we will begin an examination of several important figures that, although they might not have completely identified themselves with the label Transcendentalist, nevertheless were sufficiently influenced by, or perhaps so influential within in the Movement, that they deserve to be discussed in this series of lectures.

The first such individual is Frederick Douglass, fugitive slave, abolitionist, free thinker and eventual advisor to presidents. Indeed, Douglass met many of the leading Transcendentalist figures during the time that he lectured in and around Boston and Concord. More important, I think, Douglass's own life came to be seen as a perfect embodiment of a wide range of Transcendentalist ideals. He was a runaway slave and also a leader of the Underground Railroad, largely self-educated and yet, he went on to become a bestselling author and eventually a counselor to Abraham Lincoln.

He also began the publication of *The North Star*, one of the most widely circulated and influential abolitionist periodicals during the same year that the first Woman's Rights Convention was held at Seneca Falls in New York, a convention that Douglass also attended. As a lecturer, as an editor, as a campaigner for women's rights and even as a political appointee, Douglass revealed that the power of one person's ideas might become the embodied truth of an entire social movement.

Frederick Douglass, it is fair to say, was a sort of Martin Luther King, Jr., for the 19th century. By turns, he was a public speaker and author, an editor, an activist, and perhaps most of all, what we would have to call a civil rights campaigner. Douglass's life and his words have often been seen as a living example of many of the ideals of the New England Transcendentalists.

Let me explain what I mean when I say that. As a runaway slave, he was virtually self-educated and by now we realize that that notion fits in perfectly with Transcendentalist beliefs about the power of the innate individual and about the sense of some people who have an intuitive and direct connection, not only with the world, but with all of the larger truth around them. But in Douglass's case his journalism and his lecturing also came to connect him with what we might call the emerging media of his time, giving him a wide public platform and a large number of individuals who waited for the publication of the next edition of his journal or who flocked, in large numbers, to hear his public speeches.

His life and his work as an abolitionist came to stand, as we will see, for the moralist as a powerful individual above all else. In fact, in Douglass's case, he ended up breaking with both William Lloyd Garrison and with John Brown in favor of the power of his own vision. He was never seeking to find the individual or the group with which he could ally himself. Douglass was not only a self-made person, he was also a self-sustaining and once again, in Emerson's phrase, a very "self-reliant" individual.

By the time of his death, at the end of the 19th century, he had come to represent, in the minds of literally thousands of people, the authority of a single soul who might try to bring about, and indeed helped to bring about, sweeping social changes. In the course of Douglass's long public career, he lectured not only in Boston, but also in the smaller town of Concord and managed to meet not only Emerson and Thoreau, but also figures such as Dr. Channing, the elder, and Theodore Parker. Indeed Emerson himself had spoken out in public against slavery for the first time as early as 1844, and by 1851, Emerson was willing to attack the Fugitive Slave Law in front of an assembled public audience in Concord. Here is how Emerson's attack was presented, "An immoral law makes it a man's duty to break it [...] Let us respect the Union to all honest ends. But also respect an older and wider union, the law of Nature and rectitude."

There again we find a very similar principle to the one Thoreau would express in "Civil Disobedience," the idea that we would respect public laws and political rules up to a certain point, but that we had a higher duty to break an individual law if it contravened what Emerson here calls the "law of Nature," and rectitude, rightness.

Emerson concluded, and many abolitionists came to agree with him, that any law that would lead to the recapture of runaway slaves need to be "wiped out of the statute-book; but whilst it stands there, it must be disobeyed." There again, the moral principle, the law, as Emerson says, needs to be wiped out of the statute book, but as long as it remains a law, we, as individual moral consciences, are required to break that law.

Douglass had in fact, initially joined with those Concordians we talked about, who supported John Brown and, in fact, Douglass became a confidante of Brown's up until the time of the Harpers Ferry raid, at which point Douglass's opinions changed in ways I shall describe shortly.

Douglass's great public power derived, I think, initially from the effect of his oratory, from his ability as a public speaker. His earliest speeches dealt mainly with his own personal experiences and in fact, they were rendered with such powerful rhetorical skill and with such emotional enthusiasm, that some people refused to believe he had actually been a slave. Many people found it hard to imagine that someone raised in the conditions of slavery had managed to produce a speech that could be delivered with such elevated diction and such a powerfully intellectual argument.

Those who heard him speak almost always reported on this power of his oratory, in the same way people did of Emerson. Douglass, in early speeches, was willing to describe slave owners beating slaves of every sort; he described, for example, a young girl's head, covered with festering sores. He would not turn his eyes away from the most sordid aspects of the institution of slavery. He even discussed in detail the practice of breeding slaves as though they were prized animals. These were remarkable facts for him to present before public audiences and, in fact, some of these details of the institution of slavery were news, at that time, to many Northerners.

Let me read you a long passage from perhaps Douglass's most important work, and as I am reading, I ask you to cast your mind back to the 1840s and consider what effect these words would have had on you, as a member of a white audience or perhaps as a runaway slave, or even a slave who was still suffering under that institution. Here is how Douglass remembered the details of some of his earlier life:

> I have often been awakened at the dawn of day by the most heart-rending shrieks of an own aunt of mine, whom Mr. Plummer used to tie up to a joist, and whip upon her naked back till she was literally covered with blood. No words, no tears, no prayers from his gory victim, seemed to move his iron heart from its bloody purpose. The louder she screamed, the harder he whipped; and where the blood ran fastest, there he whipped longest. He would whip her to make her scream,

and whip her to make her hush; and not until overcome by fatigue, would he cease to swing the blood-clotted cowskin.

That is even a difficult passage to read 150 years later and it does not take much imagination for us to appreciate the effect that passages like that would have had on public audiences when Douglass was speaking extemporaneously, or on readers, when they began to read his works in print.

But Douglass was even willing to use humor to good effect, as almost all great orators have been able to do. For example, he often retold the moment when, as he said, he "broke the slave breaker" named Edward Covey by fighting back. Of course, for a slave to fight back was almost an unheard of response at this time. Likewise, he offered an apparently laughable imitation of clergymen in their pulpits who promised slaves that God would be angered if they dared to disobey their owners and masters. Douglass was able to go through an entire range of emotions in order to bring his audience around to his powerful point of view. From his birth into slavery, up until his death as a fully international figure, Douglass fought tirelessly for the rights of all black Americans, and from early on, he linked those rights to the rights of all human beings, another important factor that I think helped to tie him to the Transcendentalists.

He was born, as I have said, a slave on the Eastern Shore of Maryland in 1818. He was the son actually, of a white man and a slave woman, whom he saw only several times during his life. This was not an entirely unusual situation for a person such as Douglass at this era in history. He escaped once earlier in his life and was recaptured. This is an event that he recorded in his autobiographical writings, as perhaps one of his most terrible experiences. He creates a powerful sense of that feeling of freedom suddenly achieved by the runaway slave and then taken away during his recapture. Given both the Underground Railroad and the eventual Fugitive Slave Law, we can see why that image would also become a powerful part of his oratory.

He actually escaped for good when he was 20 years old by impersonating a sailor. However, it is also important, as we continue this lecture, to realize that in certain places Douglass was still considered a fugitive for decades, until the Civil War ended.

Throughout a large part of his early career, while his public persona was building, there were still places in America where Douglass was in fear for his own personal freedom in terms of any public appearances.

Douglass had met a free black woman named Anna Murray while he was still in slavery, and after his successful runaway, they married and moved north to Massachusetts to begin a family. It was clearly that move to Massachusetts that helped to bring Frederick Douglass into this remarkable circle of people that we have been discussing.

It was not long after his arrival in Massachusetts that he lectured for the first time to the Massachusetts Anti-Slavery Society, where he met William Lloyd Garrison, at that point, probably the best-known abolitionist in America. Douglass's career as a public speaker, and quickly thereafter as a writer, flourished. In many ways, I think it was because a former slave could speak and could write with accuracy and with a conviction that would have been very hard to achieve on the part of a white lecturer or writer. There was something not only about the power of Douglass's oratory, but also about the authenticity with which he could describe all of these events, that both drew people who were sympathetic to him, and which made everything he said utterly convincing.

He began an important related career in 1847, when he published, for the first time, *The North Star*. In a way, this was a weekly that set out to rival Garrison's publication called *The Liberator*. This was a case, as I have suggested, where Douglass seems to have wanted to separate his ideas from those of others. Douglass's masthead for his own publication, *The North Star*, is worth quoting. He placed his motto here, immediately under the title of the newspaper. Here is what the motto said, "Right is of no sex—Truth is of no color—God is the Father of us all, and we are all Brethren." There, in a short sentence, Douglass's idea is summarized.

In 1848, a year later, he attended the first convention for women's rights that was held at Seneca Falls and there he linked the struggles of slaves with the struggles of oppressed women. He also traveled as far as England, where he claimed later to have felt fully free for the first time and where he went on to link the rights of slaves to the rights of oppressed people of all kinds. Slavery had ended much earlier in the 1820s in England, so I think that accounts both for the different feeling that Douglass would have had among people in

England and also for his ability to take his own concerns for the rights of black Americans and link them with oppressed people everywhere.

While he was in England, his lectures came to support women, Irish Home Rule and even the Temperance Movement. Indeed, he would return to England later in his life when he was worried about being linked to John Brown's raid and execution. As I said, when John Brown made his raid on Harpers Ferry, Douglass felt the need to separate himself from the sympathy he had had for Brown earlier in Brown's own abolitionist career, and it is clear that Douglass's departure for England, for a second time, later in his life, was partly tied to wanting to separate himself from those terrifying events.

By the time of the Civil War, Douglass was enough of a public figure to be called to the White House for meetings with Abraham Lincoln. In fact, Lincoln eventually came to refer to him as "my friend Douglass." At this point in his career, Douglass was a widely known and widely appreciated figure and it is clear that Douglass actually gave Lincoln advice that Lincoln took very seriously. These were not just opportunities for Lincoln to ally himself with this well known public individual.

We know that because Douglass's own influence helped him to become a recruiter for black soldiers during the Civil War, eventually totaling about two companies of individuals, including two of Douglass's own sons. Douglass was actually involved in efforts to support the war in human terms. He even went on to meet with Andrew Johnson after the Civil War had ended to discuss the rights of former slaves and all of the complex series of issues that surrounded reconstruction.

After the end of the Civil War, Douglass actively supported all of those constitutional amendments that made equal rights a matter of law; it was not just a question for him that slavery had formally ended. Douglass, as well as many individuals, realized the important issues that still confronted the nation in terms of what would happen to former slaves in the South and about how that series of issues surrounding reconstruction would be resolved most effectively.

The issue of course, as we know from histories of reconstruction, was by no means settled in a short period of time. Douglass, throughout his later life, lamented the lack of any real opportunities for black people in America, and he consistently bemoaned the continued separation of the races. He became, in a sense, an embodiment of a whole series of ideals that may have been practically realized with the end of the Civil War, but which, as we know, continue even into our own era.

He was also important, at this point in his life, for continually claiming that racism was not merely "a southern problem." He was not one of those figures who wanted solely to demonize the South, but clearly, given his own experiences as an African-American lucky enough to move easily through North and South, especially after the war had ended, Douglass clearly felt the stings of racism that still pervaded the whole society.

After the Civil War, Douglass wrote a well known passage about John Brown that I think, once again, helps to give us a sense of how conflicted people's feelings were about Brown, in this case especially powerfully rendered because the words come from the mouth of a former slave. Here is what Douglass said, "Did John Brown fail? […] John Brown began the war that ended American slavery and made this a free Republic. […] His zeal in the cause of my race was far greater than mine."

We may imagine the second part of this quotation to be something of a rhetorical exaggeration, but it is clear that Douglass wanted to make the point about the intensity of emotions that were required in order to deal with ongoing racial issues.

Late in his own life, and after the death of his first wife, Douglass married his white former secretary. He silenced a number of his critics of this marriage by saying—once again, I think with a note of humor—that his mother's race had been honored by his first marriage; and now his father's race would be honored by his second marriage. He was even able to silence critics of his biracial marriage with a reference to his own personal autobiography.

The legacy of Douglass was widespread and powerful in America and beyond, not only during his life, but also well after his own lifetime. His writings were almost always immediate bestsellers and he continued to speak out publicly on all of those causes that concerned him until the virtual end of his life.

His first book, published in 1845, and still his best known, was the *Narrative of the Life of Frederick Douglass, An American Slave*,

©2006 The Teaching Company Limited Partnership

written by him. Then in a book entitled *My Bondage, My Freedom*, published 10 years later in 1855, Douglass went on to describe that first trip to England that I have mentioned. He also added an extremely important lecture and essay that he had written entitled "What to the Slave is the Fourth of July?" "What to the Slave is the Fourth of July?" became almost a rallying cry for those followers of Douglass, especially after the Civil War and I would like, again, to read a long passage from this work in order to suggest both the power of Douglass's oratory, but also the way he links the specific contents of his own experience to much wider social concerns. Here is the passage:

> The blessings in which you, this day, rejoice, are not enjoyed in common. The rich inheritance of justice, liberty, prosperity and independence, bequeathed by your fathers, is shared by you, not by me. The sunlight that brought life and healing to you, has brought stripes and death to me. This Fourth [of] July is yours, not mine. You may rejoice, I must mourn. To drag a man in fetters into the grand illuminated temple of liberty, and call upon him to join you in joyous anthems, were inhuman mockery and sacrilegious irony.

In this passage we have a powerful sense of the way Douglass is always unwilling to hold back. He pushes the logic of his argument as far as possible and uses a powerful metaphor; in this case we have to describe it as a poetically imaginative image of a man, in this case we imagine Douglass himself, being dragged in chains, as he says, "into the temple of liberty." He says there is nothing for a black person to celebrate about this, this is only "mockery and sacrilegious irony." This speech was delivered before the Civil War, but as I have suggested, the rhetorical fervor that it embodies and its sense of who the blessings of liberty actually apply to in America, certainly continued to be a powerful question in the public realm long after the Civil War.

In 1881, Douglass finally published the third of his autobiographical volumes, this time called simply *Life and Times of Frederick Douglass*. In effect, what Douglass did in these three volumes was to publish versions of his autobiography on each separate occasion, but each subsequent volume added more details and, as we might expect by now, more candor. As Douglass's own public reputation grew, he was ever more willing to express his ideas with energy and fervor, partly because his own fame helped to secure him from attacks by others and because I think he understood the power of the position that he came to occupy in American history. There is almost no other figure in the 19th century who had either the biographical arc represented by Douglass's life or who was thought of in such profoundly respectful terms by everyone, from those newly freed slaves after the Civil War, who perhaps finally were able to read Douglass for the first time, all the way, as I have suggested, to the presidents of the United States.

Many people—then and now—have celebrated Douglass, either in words or in their own lives. The poet, Paul Laurence Dunbar, for example, had a wonderful couple of lines about Douglass. Dunbar said, "To sin and crime he gave their proper hue,/And hurled at evil what was evil's due."

There is a sense, even in those two lines of poetry, of the powerful energy of Douglass's life history, the sense of actually hurling at evil what evil required and as a result, being able to defeat certain aspects of evil's actions.

Douglass's "What to the Slave is the Fourth of July?" has actually often been compared to Martin Luther King's "I Have a Dream" speech. In the case of Douglass's work, not in terms of the kind of optimism we might associate with King's "I Have a Dream," but rather in recognition, in King's words, "of the withering injustice" at the heart of American democracy and of a continuing "lonely island of poverty in the midst of a vast ocean of material prosperity." Those are King's words again, but they suggest very strongly that feeling that Douglass also echoed, that even once the political realities of slavery had been dealt with, the Transcendentalist ideal of absolute human freedom was still a dream.

Finally, I think, Douglass wanted to make the grand promise of America available to all of America's citizens. From my point of view, the work of his legacy clearly continues.

From here we will move to look at Emily Dickinson.

Lecture Twenty-One
Emily Dickinson

Scope:

Emily Dickinson is a figure who, like Frederick Douglass, might not have called herself a Transcendentalist, but her work cannot be fully understood without reference to the circle of people who surrounded her in Transcendentalist literary circles and in Massachusetts. She read Emerson's poems and often noted their influence on her thinking. She admired Thoreau throughout her life. Her literary work, like theirs, consistently relies on an emphasis on the contents of individual consciousness. Language in her poems is a tool for direct understanding of reality via sensuous perception of the physical world. Of course, Dickinson was also one of those figures who sought a new version of spirituality, one that linked the material world closely to the immaterial and one that credited human psychology with the origin of our individualized human views of the world. In her wrenching of language into new symbolic meanings and her reliance on her own ideas as keys to understanding, Dickinson embodies central tenets of the Transcendentalists that surrounded her.

Outline

I. Emily Dickinson's (1830–1886) poetry intersects at important points with numerous ideas linked to New England Transcendentalism.

   A. Her individualism is her own, but it also owes much—especially early on—to the influence of Emerson.

   1. In 1850, Dickinson received Emerson's first collection of *Poems* from a friend, including the bardic voice of "Give All to Love" ("When half-gods go,/The gods arrive") and naturalistic poems, such as "The Humblebee" ("Wiser far than human seer,/Yellow-breeched philosopher!").

   2. Many of her later poems echo his themes directly: nature, death, knowledge, selfhood.

   3. In 1857 Emerson visited Amherst for a lecture and stayed with Dickinson's brother and sister-in-law, although Dickinson proved too shy and retiring to venture out to meet him.

4. She often stressed an Emersonian emphasis on nonconformity, as in her famous "Much Madness is Divinest Sense": "Assent, and you are Sane;/Demur,—you're straightway dangerous,/And handled with a Chain."

B. Many critics have also noted Dickinson's connection to the ideas of Thoreau.

1. Her recent biographer, Alfred Habegger, notes that Thoreau may have been the subject of "Twas fighting for his Life he was—":

> I dwell in Possibility—
> A fairer House than Prose—
> More numerous of Windows—
> Superior—for Doors—
>
> Of Chambers as the Cedars—
> Impregnable of Eye—
> And for an Everlasting Roof
> The Gambrels of the Sky—
>
> Of Visitors—the fairest
> For Occupation—This—
> The spreading wide my narrow Hands
> To gather Paradise— (c. 1862)

2. Her religious skepticism, even more thoroughgoing than that of most Transcendentalists, can also be compared to Thoreau's, whose church was always described as out of doors, as in,

> Some keep the Sabbath going to Church—
> I keep it, staying at Home—
> With a Bobolink for a Chorister—
> And an Orchard, for a Dome—

C. Dickinson's preoccupation with death links her more closely to Herman Melville, usually a critic of Transcendentalism.

1. "Because I could not stop for Death/He kindly stopped for me."

2. Her life and her work can been linked to the Romantic ideas that the good are too good for this world, the artist is a hermit, and the good die young.
3. Her own life provides a model of the Romantic artist, isolated and separated from society, almost "dead" to the world, but nevertheless producing lasting works of art that have a direct impact on society at large.

II. Dickinson's literary work, like that of almost all of the greatest authors, is significant for its revolutionary style, as well as its remarkable substance.

A. On the surface, she often seems more Puritanical than the reform-minded Transcendentalists.
   1. The structure and meter of hymns is one of the only obvious traditional sources for her lyrics.
   2. She was clearly influenced by English Metaphysical poets of the 1600s.
   3. More important, perhaps, emotions as strong as Emily Bronte's or Emerson's linked her to the struggle to break away from Puritanical, Calvinist New England.
   4. Once we get below the surface of many of her poems, we see a robust vitality, a sensuous apprehension of the physical world, and an almost Modernist attention to personal experience:

   > A bird came down the walk:
   > He did not know I saw;
   > He bit an angle-worm in halves
   > And ate the fellow, raw.
   >
   > And then he drank a dew
   > From a convenient grass,
   > And then hopped sidewise to the wall
   > To let a beetle pass.

B. Dickinson also invents new forms of language for the expression of her ideas.
   1. Her grammar is often strained, stretched, and forced into new structures.
   2. She uses dashes, rhetorical ellipses, and breaks to suggest the immediacy of mental activity.

3. Her vocabulary and rhetoric are often marshaled like ammunition for a literary weapon that is poetry.

C. Her poems develop a psychological approach to reality that anticipates modern developments in the study of language and literary theory.

    1. The use of nature in Dickinson's poems derives not only from Emerson but from her personal fascination with botany, geology, and astronomy, as well as the influence of Darwin after 1859.

    2. Her strange, reclusive life has made her the subject of extensive speculation about her love life, her sexuality, and her precise feelings for those around her.

    3. Dickinson's determined individualism was tied to her private but prodigious literary life. She wrote roughly 1,800 poems but published only seven during her lifetime. As a result, dating the poems precisely is almost impossible, since editors have had to rely solely on the small bundles, often called "fascicles," into which Dickinson collected her undated groups of poems.

    4. Her lyrics remind us that each of us can be a maker of the language we use, rather than merely a passive recipient of the language around us.

III. Dickinson's influence has made her a cultural icon as much for her way of life as for the literary masterpieces she produced.

A. Her first-person, relentlessly autobiographical speaker is a very modern poetic voice, poised in the present moment and almost preternaturally sensitive to the nuances of surrounding sensations.

    1. She has been compared, for example, to Ezra Pound and T. S. Eliot.

    2. Sylvia Plath, in the 20th century, has had a similar influence on female poets and literary feminism in America.

    3. The struggle in Dickinson between Puritanism and Transcendentalism echoes a wider struggle in the American psyche. Today, we might see this as the debate between fundamentalism and liberalism, which is not merely a religious issue.

B. We now think of the "Belle of Amherst" as a much more complex person than earlier descriptions of her suggested.

    1. The housebound spinster has been replaced by a person vividly alive with an inner life and frustrated by the hypocrisy and triviality of most of what passed for meaningful life in the public world.

    2. The modern artist is often, like Dickinson, an inner seer, one who offers a poetics of identity by combining self-denial with self-assertion.

    3. Dickinson's version of Transcendentalism offers a unified vision that is not part of a system but, rather, immediate personal experience transformed into meaningful art. She is a quintessentially American artist.

Essential Reading:

Habegger, Alfred. *My Wars Are Laid Away in Books: The Life of Emily Dickinson.*

Buell, Lawrence. "Emersonian Anti-Mentoring: From Thoreau to Dickinson and Beyond."

Supplementary Reading:

Diehl, Joanne Feit. "Emerson, Dickinson, and the Abyss."

Questions to Consider:

1. Emily Dickinson would probably never have called herself a Transcendentalist; why then is it appropriate to study her in a series of lectures like this one?

2. What do you find to be uniquely American about the form and content of Dickinson's poems?

Lecture Twenty-One—Transcript
Emily Dickinson

Welcome back. Now we will turn to perhaps an unlikely Transcendentalist, the poet, Emily Dickinson. Emily Dickinson is a figure who, like Frederick Douglass, might not have called herself a Transcendentalist, but her work cannot be fully understood without reference to the circle of people who surrounded her both in Transcendentalist literary circles, and in Massachusetts, more generally. She read Emerson's poems carefully and often noted their influence on her own thinking, if not directly on her writing. She admired Thoreau throughout her life. Her literary work, like theirs, consistently relies on an emphasis on the contents of her own individual consciousness.

Language, in Dickinson's poems, is a tool for direct understanding of reality, as I will try to explain, via the sensuous perception of the physical world. Of course, Dickinson was also one of those figures who sought a new version of spirituality, one that linked the material world closely to the immaterial world and one that credited our own human psychology with the origin of each individualized human view of the world. In her wrenching of our language into new symbolic meanings, and also in her reliance on her own ideas as a key to more general understanding, Dickinson embodies central tenets of those Transcendentalists that surrounded her.

Emily Dickinson's poetry intersects at a number of important points, with numerous ideas linked to those we have been discussing in this series of lectures. Her individualism is clearly her own, but it also owed much, especially early on in her life, to the influence of Ralph Waldo Emerson.

In 1850, she received Emerson's first collection of *Poems* from a friend, including that emerging bardic voice we have discussed, as for example, in Emerson's "Give All to Love," when he reminds us that "When half-gods go,/The gods arrive," suggesting that as soon as our own human-created visions of God disappear, we are closer to the truth behind divinity. Or his wonderful poem, "The Humblebee," in which he describes the creature that we would call a bumble bee in the following lines, "Wiser far than human seer,/Yellow-breeched philosopher!"

It was a bit of an Emersonian exaggeration there to call the bumble bee a philosopher. On the other hand, a clear naturalistic attempt to suggest that we should all be paying more close attention to all of the details that surround us, especially in the natural world. Many of Dickinson's later poems echo Emersonian themes directly—themes of nature, of knowledge, of selfhood and especially, I think, in Dickinson's case, the theme of death, as we will see.

In 1857, Emerson actually visited Amherst where Dickinson lived, for a lecture at Amherst College, and he stayed with Dickinson's brother and sister-in-law; although Emily proved far too shy and retiring, as her general public image suggests, to even venture out in order to meet him, so the one opportunity for these two great intellects to have met one another passed.

She did often stress a very Emersonian emphasis on nonconformity throughout her writing and in many ways, as we look at the details of her life, we will see that she actually was a much thorough-going nonconformist than Emerson ever became, as in her famous "Much Madness is Divinest Sense." In that wonderful poem she said, "Assent, and you are Sane;/Demur,—you're straightway dangerous,/And handled with a Chain."

That sense that if we go along with the crowd, if we accept the status quo, then we are defined as saying as soon as we step aside, as soon as we demur from the rules of those around us, we are immediately described as dangerous individuals and they run and find the chain to control us. It is a powerfully physical image for the person we often think of as the delicate "Belle of Amherst;" but more about that in a moment.

Many critics, especially in recent years, have noted Dickinson's connection to the ideas of Thoreau. In fact, one of her most recent biographers, Alfred Habegger, notes that Thoreau is likely to have been the subject of a poem of hers entitled "'Twas fighting for his Life he was—," once again, a very dramatic title, especially when we think of it in the context of the description it goes on to offer. Here is the entire poem:

> I dwell in Possibility—
> A fairer House than Prose—
> More numerous of Windows—
> Superior—for Doors—

Of Chambers as the Cedars—
Impregnable of Eye—
And for an Everlasting Roof
The Gambrels of the Sky—

Of Visitors—the fairest
For Occupation—This—
The spreading wide my narrow Hands
To gather Paradise—

It was written around 1862, which means she would have had the opportunity to read *Walden* by this time, and it is clear that Habegger's connection to Thoreau is based on the notion that the house this individual lives in is irrelevant, much as the cabin at Walden itself was not a significant feature. In fact, what dominates this poem is the powerful sense of cedars, the trees outside of the dwelling, as the most significant walls of a room and, as she says, the "Everlasting Roof" of this dwelling place is actually the "Gambrels of the Sky." Then finally, this powerful notion she might easily have drawn from Thoreau, that the "only visitor I need," in a sense, "is my own sense of myself," as we have discussed in considering Thoreau and "all I have to do is spread 'wide my narrow Hands'" as the final line tells us, in order to gather paradise. Whether or not this lyric refers directly to Thoreau, it clearly captures a number of images and a series of ideas that we can closely associate with ideas like his that influenced her.

Dickinson's religious skepticism, even more thorough going than many of the Transcendentalists, can also be compared to Thoreau, whose images of the church, as in this poem I have just discussed, are almost always described as out of doors. Here is another example from Dickinson, in which she associates images that we ordinarily connect only with the church building or with formal religious observations, directly with a powerful experience of the natural world. Here is Dickinson:

Some keep the Sabbath going to Church—
I keep it, staying at Home—
With a Bobolink for a Chorister—
And an Orchard, for a Dome—

Very short, very direct; that sense of almost breaking the thought of language as needed. Others go to church in order to keep the Sabbath

©2006 The Teaching Company Limited Partnership

day, "I do not need to go anywhere," says the speaker of the poem. "The only choir I need is the Bobolink," a very common woodland and meadowland bird of the New England natural scene. "And the only Dome I need over my head is an orchard." Once again, we see a series of connections between a pure and powerful experience of the natural world and something very much like spirituality.

Dickinson's preoccupation with death, which I will talk more about later, links her more closely to Herman Melville, than to most of the other Transcendentalists. Melville, as we have seen, often a critic of Transcendentalism, who was worried about that optimistic strain, especially in Emerson. Two of Dickinson's most famous lines are, "Because I could not stop for Death/He kindly stopped for me."

In a number of her poems, she personifies death powerfully as an individual or she places herself almost in the position of being beyond the grave in order to utter her own poems. This was not uncommon, especially among women poets of the 19th century. I am thinking of someone such as Christina Rossetti. But Dickinson often seems to locate her voice almost outside of, or beyond, life and the way that she does that metaphorically is by placing the voice almost in the realm of the dead.

In this sense, her life and her work can be linked to Romantic ideas that the good are sometimes too good for this world, that is to say the good die young, and also that the artist is a hermit. The artist is someone who has a vision that separates her from the world of the rest of us and in a sense, the artist is not going to be able to survive an ordinary lifespan, partly because of either the intensity of their vision or because their goodness renders them so different from the majority of people around them that they will not survive to live a full lifespan.

Indeed, Dickinson's own life came to provide a model of this Romantic artist, isolated from those around her, separate from society—as a poet might have said, almost "dead" to the world. In Dickinson's case of course, what is perhaps not surprising, given the intensity of her own awareness of her surroundings, is that she was nevertheless able to produce powerfully lasting works of art that went on not during her lifetime in any way, but certainly since her lifetime, to have a direct and powerful impact on the wider society.

Dickinson's literary work, as almost all of the greatest authors, is significant for a revolutionary style in terms of her use of language, as well as for its remarkable substance, the subject matter that she decides to include in almost all of her poems. On the surface, many have noted that she often seems more puritanical than the reform-minded Transcendentalists. What I mean by that is she often seems more concerned either with a sense of guilt or with a sense of secrets that the speaker of her poem is, in fact, hiding from the wider world. This would not fit very well with the Transcendentalist idea of feeling fully confident to express your ideas. In that sense there is a puritanical strain that remains in Dickinson, but I think it remains largely intentioned with the more transcendental aspects of her writing.

The structure and meter in fact, of traditional hymns is one of the obvious and one of the only traditional sources for the way that she structures her lyrics. She was also clearly influenced by the English metaphysical poets of the 1600s, authors such as John Donne and George Herbert, who had intense religious visions and who almost felt the need to stretch and strain and break the language in order to give full justice to the power of their thinking.

I think more important, perhaps, than either of these direct influence is that an emotional intensity, certainly as strong as Emerson's and perhaps even as strong as a writer such as Emily Brontë, actually links Dickinson to struggle to break away from that puritanical Calvinist aspect of New England in much the same way that the Transcendentalists sought to break away, but more often in purely theological or religious matters. In Dickinson, we have this feeling of someone who is trying to wrench her own thoughts and her language out of a series of traditional structures and that helps to account for part of the power that she injects into her poetry.

What I mean to suggest here is that once we go below the surface in a number of her poems, we see a robust vitality. It is a really sensuous apprehension of her physical surroundings and it is, I would have to say, Modernist. It is an almost-20th-century attention to personal experience, as distinct from trying to convey any specific message or meaning within the confines of the poem. Let me give a powerful example of this tendency in her poetry:

> A bird came down the walk:
> He did not know I saw;

He bit an angle-worm in halves
And ate the fellow, raw.

And then he drank a dew
From a convenient grass,
And then hopped sidewise to the wall
To let a beetle pass.

What is striking here is how Dickinson takes a remarkable ordinary experience, the experience of watching a bird come along, snip a worm in half and eat it; then take a drink of water and almost hop to let a beetle pass by on the sidewalk. What is striking here is the way the language itself turns this into a memorable experience because it gives us an image that we have a hard time getting out of our head, once it is planted in there, partly because of the careful attention she gives to tone: "He bit an angle-worm in halves," that is fine, we can follow that as a description. But then, "And ate the fellow, raw;" simply by referring to the worm as a "fellow" and reminding us that animals tend to eat each other in the state of being raw, she gives a powerfully instantaneous vision of exactly what she is seeing.

Of course, what is also significant by the time we reach the end of these lines, and the bird simply hops to the side to let the beetle walk by, once again, the diction almost diminishes what seems to be the seriousness of the scene. But unlike so much 19th-century poetry, Dickinson offers us no conclusion about what this experience means. That would be what would cause me to connect this with Modernist writing. What Dickinson seems to say is, "You make of this experience what you will?" You put this image into your consciousness as a function of her description, and then you decide why this experience is valuable, or even what it might mean. In that sense, she often distinguishes herself from 19th-century writing, especially poetry, that is trying to convey an ethical message, that is trying to leave us with a neatly tied-up moral and she, instead, presents her own experience, as I like to say. As so many of the greatest poets, what she really does in a lyric like this is simply to give us back the world. In doing that, she makes this image of the world memorable.

But Dickinson also invents a new form of language for the expression of these powerful ideas. Her grammar—as critics have noted since her poems first came into circulation, only after her death widely—her grammar is often strained and stretched and pushed into new structures. She uses dashes almost without a sense of any necessary rule about where the dash will appear. She uses rhetorical ellipses, breaks in the syntax and as I have tried to argue, just the immediacy of our own mental activity by being willing to break any rule of language in order to give us a sense of what it felt like to see something. What the sound of a particular natural object or event hitting her ear actually conveyed into her mind.

Both her vocabulary and her rhetoric, I think, are often marshaled almost like ammunition. It is as though she has a weapon that she is going to deploy in order to make sure that we understand precisely what she has experienced, and her weapon, of course, is poetry. In this I think she anticipates a lot of 20th-century and even 21st-century writing that has been willing to sacrifice the rules of language in order to move us ever closer to the experience itself.

In this regard, Dickinson's poems develop a psychological approach to reality that actually anticipates not only a series of modern developments in the study of language, but also in literary theory. The use of nature in her poetry derives not only from Emerson, but with Dickinson's own personal fascination with botany, with geology and even with astronomy as well as the influence of Darwin after 1859. She is one of the earliest poets in the language—the only example in England would perhaps be Tennyson—in America Dickinson is one of the earliest poets to actually echo and appreciate the influence of Darwin on her own thinking about the natural world.

Of course, her strange and reclusive life—the cliché of course, is that Emily almost never left her house in Amherst—but the strange and reclusive life has made her the subject of extensive speculation, especially in recent times, about her love life, about her sexuality and about her precise feelings for those around her. One of the interesting things, again, about her poetry and this connection to more Modernist ideas about the way language actually operates, is that even when her poems are being autobiographical, we do not have an immediate sense of their connection to a specific set of circumstances.

In psychological terms, she is also so willing to go through the entire range of her emotional responses to events that we have the sense that we are actually hearing the voices of more than one person, perhaps even in the same poem, and that certainly she is presenting her own personality in a very rich and layered and textured fashion that we are certainly not used to in the case of 19th-century poets, and once again, takes us much closer to the searing honesty that we associate with much later writings.

This same determined individualism of hers was tied to her very private, but also her prodigious literary life. It is fair to say that Emily was a reclusive person, almost a hermit. Certainly she had a private side to her character that she never revealed anywhere except in her writings. It is really quite remarkable, even to this day, to consider that she wrote roughly 1,800 poems, but only published seven of them during her lifetime. Imagine any poet today who would spend a lifetime producing close to 2,000 separate lyrics, who would chose to publish only seven of them in the public arena.

As a result of this, the dating of her poems, especially individual poems to precise dates, is almost impossible since editors after her death were only able to rely on small bundles that Emily herself collected. Nowadays, and since her early editors, these bundles are most often called fascicles; these are the groups into which she collected her otherwise undated groups of poems. Once again, our attempts to connect specific aspects of her biography to specific poems were very much thwarted until only recent years, when scholars began to sit down and try to associate each undated poem with an event in her life or with a change in her way of thinking.

I think the important aspect of this phenomenon for us to take away, especially in terms of her link to Transcendentalism, is that this fascinating and remarkable collection of lyrics remind us that each of us can be a maker of the language that we use rather than merely the passive recipient of the public language we find around us.

All of the great writers in history, whether it was Chaucer, Shakespeare, Milton or Dickinson, have tended to participate in this ability to create new aspects or new forms of language. What Dickinson's poetry does for us, I think, is to remind us that each human being has the power to take the force of his or her own experience and shape language that will describe it as accurately as possible. In that sense, I think her influence goes beyond the purely poetic, into—as I have suggested—aspects of literary theory, but also even beyond those questions into each person's own individual response to language.

Dickinson's influence has made her a cultural icon, as much for her way of life as for the series of literary masterpieces she was able to produce. Her frequent first-person, and relentlessly autobiographical, speaker is a very modern poetic voice, as I have tried to argue. It is almost always poised in the present moment and it is what I would have to call preternaturally sensitive to each nuance of her surrounding sensations. What I mean is she even seems to go beyond the sensuous awareness brought to her by her five senses, into the actual processes of thought with which she is taking in the sensations that surround her.

She has been compared to Ezra Pound and to T. S. Eliot in this regard who, once again, were willing to break the rules of ordinary language and certainly to break the accepted standards of poetic convention in order to move themselves and their readers closer to individual personal experience.

Sylvia Plath, in the 20th century, has had, I think, a similar influence on female poets and on what we would have to call literary feminism in America. I do not think it is insignificant that Dickinson was one of the few female voices in the 19th century—even though she had no public presence until after her death—she was one of the few female voices who was able to give poetic language to female experience, not only as distinct from male experience, but as part of a common human experience.

What I have already described as the struggle in her between Puritanism and Transcendentalism seems to echo an even wider struggle in the American psyche. Today we might see this as connected to the debate between fundamentalism, that would be the Puritan strain, and liberalism, that would be the Transcendentalist strain, and I mean those words, "fundamentalist" and "liberal" not merely in a religious sense or a political sense. What I am suggesting is that Dickinson clearly understood those parts of her character that held her back from certain kinds of public engagement and that kept her feeling restrained and restricted, partly as a woman, certainly as a female poet and in some ways, as anyone alive in the 19th century must have felt restrained by either social expectations, religious convention or all the things that we have seen these Transcendentalist thinkers trying, in some sense, to break away from.

Again and again in her poetry, we find this willingness to challenge an accepted way of thinking or to present an aspect of experience that seems to stand on its own without needing to be explained or to fit into a wider context.

As a result of these kinds of thoughts, we now imagine the Belle of Amherst, as she has often been called, as a much more complex person than earlier descriptions of her suggested. The image of the housebound spinster who was in a sense cloistered away, simply penning her isolated and somewhat frustrated lyrics has been vividly replaced by a person alive, with a powerful inner life, frustrated by the hypocrisy and the triviality of a great deal of what passed for meaningful life in the public world outside of her.

The modern artist in fact, is often, as Dickinson, a kind of inner seer; that is to say a person who offers what I like to call a poetics of identity, by combining the aspects of self-denial—which we all feel—with powerful aspects of self-assertion, which most of us aspire to.

Dickinson's own version of Transcendentalism, finally, offers a unified vision that, once again, is not part of a formal system but rather presents immediate personal experience transformed into meaningful artistic achievement. In that sense, she is a quintessentially American artist.

Now we will turn to perhaps her male counterpart as a quintessentially American artist; that is Walt Whitman.

Lecture Twenty-Two
Walt Whitman

Scope:

We will end our discussion of significant figures with Walt Whitman, a poet and thinker whose works reveal direct links to ideas that were flying from brain to brain in Concord and elsewhere during this era. Whitman's poetry is, like Dickinson's, a poetry of the individual, yet Whitman's individual is very different from Dickinson's. Whitman clearly believed that he was "The Poet" described by and hoped for by Emerson in his essay of the same name. Whitman says as much in the preface to *Leaves of Grass*, his greatest single volume of poetry. While Dickinson was willing to remain cloistered and publicly silent in her home in Amherst (her poems were scarcely known until after her death), Whitman insisted that he was a prophetic voice of, by, and for the "People." Even Whitman's poetic practice bears comparison with the Transcendentalists. He would write short snippets of immediate inspiration on slips of printer's paper, the so-called "leaves" of *Leaves of Grass*. He collected them only later and worked to organize them into a unified whole. Emerson and Thoreau both visited Whitman in New York.

Outline

I. Walt Whitman (1819–1892) saw himself as the "The Poet" described by Emerson in his 1844 essay.

    A. Emerson called for a poet who could speak for the people and who would also be a public figure in the life of the nation.

        1. Emerson lamented, "Our log-rolling, our stumps and their politics, our fisheries, our Negroes, and Indians, our boasts, and our repudiations, the wrath of rogues, and the pusillanimity of honest men, the northern trade, the southern planting, the western clearing, Oregon, and Texas, are yet unsung."

        2. Whitman echoed this sentiment by saying, in the 1855 preface to *Leaves of Grass*, "The United States themselves are essentially the greatest poem."

3. Emerson responded with a letter Whitman then quoted in the preface: "I give you joy of your free and brave thought. I have great joy in it. I find incomparable things said incomparably well [...] I greet you at the beginning of a great career."

B. Whitman has the kind of expansiveness and inclusiveness that appealed to many Transcendentalists.
   1. Whitman's career as a printer was central to his art. He personally set the type for parts of the first edition; in fact, *grass* is a term that printers use to refer to preliminary or experimental typesetting, drafts, less than final work.
   2. Transcendentalists would have applauded this link between the practical and the artistic, as well as this open-ended aesthetic.
   3. The Civil War was a shaping influence on a great deal of Whitman's verse, culminating in his elegiac masterpiece for Lincoln, "When lilacs last in the door-yard bloom'd":

   > When lilacs last in the door-yard bloom'd,
   > And the great star early droop'd in the western sky in the night,
   > I mourn'd—and yet shall mourn with ever-returning spring.
   >
   > O ever-returning spring! trinity sure to me you bring;
   > Lilac blooming perennial, and drooping star in the west,
   > And thought of him I love.

   4. *Leaves of Grass*, as a number of critics have noted, brought two new subjects into American poetry, the importance of sexuality and the value of human labor. Sex was part of nature, as the more liberal Transcendentalists had taught, and all employment was potentially noble, whether that of the lawyer, the seamstress, the ditch digger, or even the prostitute.
   5. As the critic Jerome Loving has noted:

   > The poet reasoned that if—according to transcendentalist doctrine—everyone was divine

because nature was emblematic of God, then all were equal, politically equal, including women, whom Whitman treated equally with men [...] This idea of equality and self-divinity also meant that one could celebrate himself or herself. And so the first poem of the first edition of *Leaves of Grass* began: "I celebrate myself [and sing myself]/And what I assume you shall assume,/For every atom belonging to me as good belongs to you."

    6. In that sense, he is—above all—our poet of democracy.

C. Whitman's sensuousness caused him problems throughout his career.

    1. He wrote about the human body, and about sexual desire, in ways that had rarely been attempted:

> Examine these limbs, red, black, or white—they are so cunning in tendon and nerve;
> They shall be stript, that you may see them.

> Exquisite senses, life-lit eyes, pluck, volition,
> Flakes of breast-muscle, pliant back-bone and neck,
> flesh not flabby, good-sized arms and legs,
> And wonders within there yet. ("I Sing the Body Electric")

    2. Whitman offended many, including many Transcendentalists, with his open and frank approach to sexuality: "Have you ever loved the Body of a woman?/Have you ever loved the Body of a Man?"

    3. His homosexual desire was implicit rather than explicit, but it was evident to many readers.

    4. Emerson tried to present Whitman to the respectable Saturday Club in Boston, but after such sexually explicit poems as "Enfans d'Adam" appeared in the 1860 edition of *Leaves*, Longfellow, Oliver Wendell Holmes, and others refused.

    5. Emerson, on a famous walk around Boston Common, tried to convince Whitman to tone down his overt sexuality, but even after the poet refused, Emerson remained his defender. As Whitman wrote, "I could never hear the point better put—and then I felt down in my soul the clear and unmistakable conviction to disobey all, and pursue my own way."

    D. Whitman relished the role of eccentric outsider, but he linked that role with a very American view of the individual.

        1. As Emerson had requested, Whitman clearly saw himself as a spokesman for America and for all Americans, from women to Indians to freed slaves.

        2. He knew that some of the positions he adopted would set him against culturally accepted ways of thinking and acting.

        3. Romanticism had sometimes depicted the poet as an outsider, almost too good for society, but Wordsworth, among others, had written passionately about the lives of ordinary people.

        4. Whitman may have solved the dilemma by saying, "If you want me again look for me under your boot-soles" ("Song of Myself").

        5. He called himself "a cosmos" but also "a loafer."

        6. Emerson had solved this problem earlier by saying, once again in "The Poet": "The poet is representative. He stands among partial men for the complete man, and apprises us not of his wealth, but of the commonwealth."

II. Whitman's life came to be seen as "Romantic" as his art.

    A. He was self-taught after being apprenticed to a printer at age 14; his rough-and-tumble career as a journalist prepared him for the poetry that was to come.

        1. On Long Island, he worked as an innovative schoolteacher who told his students to call him "Walt" and used games to help teach math and spelling.

        2. He traveled widely in the North and South and experienced slavery firsthand in New Orleans.

        3. His career as a journalist and editor included working for the *Brooklyn Daily Eagle*, the *New Orleans Crescent*, and a "free soil" abolitionist paper back in Brooklyn.

    B. Emerson and Thoreau visited Whitman in New York and found him a uniquely remarkable figure.

        1. Emerson visited in 1855, but when the two went to Emerson's hotel, the elegant Astor, Whitman's shabby clothes denied him entrance to Emerson's room. They met many times in the next three decades, and their relationship mixed respect with an element of suspicion.

2. Thoreau and Bronson Alcott visited Whitman a year after Emerson. Alcott recorded that each man was "surveying the other curiously, like two beasts, each wondering what the other would do."

3. Thoreau soon described him:

> That Walt Whitman, of whom I wrote to you, is the most interesting fact to me at present. […] There are two or three pieces in the book which are disagreeable, to say the least; simply sensual. […] But even on this side he has spoken more truth than any American or modern that I know. I have found his poem exhilarating, encouraging […] On the whole, it sounds to me very brave and American […] He is awfully good.

4. By the time of *Leaves of Grass* (1855), Whitman's unique style was fully formed: experimental, the long line, unrhymed, no consistent meter, journalistic, biblical, prophetic, mundane, democratic, dispersed but unifying, like America itself.

5. "Do I contradict myself?" Whitman snapped in "Song of Myself": "Very well then […] I contradict myself;/I am large […] I contain multitudes"; we again can compare Emerson: "A foolish consistency is the hobgoblin of little minds."

III. Whitman's unconventionality of style and substance can be linked to a Romantic and to a more specifically American view of the artist.

A. The idea of the unconventionality of the artist goes back at least to the Romantics, to such figures as Lord Byron and Percy Shelley, but extends in the 19th century to include such figures as Vincent van Gogh and the French Symbolists.

1. Such artistic eccentricity or excess is often seen as a sign of genius.

2. The artist is unable to fit into polite society or accepted standards of behavior.

3. Transcendentalists believe that any idea is worth scrutiny if it leads to a vision of the truth.

> 4. As Whitman, like many with Romantic sensibilities, might say, the divine can appear in even the most unlikely places; the ordinary is extraordinary.

B. Whitman's influence extends to us through many artists and ideas.

> 1. Ezra Pound, as early as 1915, declared Whitman to be a father figure of Modernism.
> 2. Poets from T. S. Eliot to William Carlos Williams to Robert Frost have agreed with Pound's high praise and have cited Whitman's influence.
> 3. With his screaming poem *Howl*, Allen Ginsberg, like other Beat poets, delivered the "barbaric yawp" ("I sound my barbaric yawp over the roofs of the world," "Song of Myself") of Whitman into the voice of postwar poetry.
> 4. Even today, we draw a similar link to rock stars and visual artists, whose life and works often leave them at the edge of polite society.
> 5. More significant than the personality of the artist, however, and like many Transcendentalists, Whitman gave voice to early versions of America's gradual progress toward racial, social, and sexual freedom.

Essential Reading:

Whitman, Walt. *Poetry and Prose*.

Kaplan, Justin. *Walt Whitman: A Life*.

Supplementary Reading:

Loving, Jerome. *Walt Whitman: Song of Himself*.

Questions to Consider:

1. Whitman calls his own poetry a "barbaric yawp." Does he mean that as a compliment to himself or an insult? Why?

2. America has arguably produced more individualistic writers than England or perhaps even Europe. Why is this the case?

Lecture Twenty-Two—Transcript
Walt Whitman

We will now end our discussion of significant figures with Walt Whitman, a poet and a thinker whose works reveal direct links to those ideas that were flying from brain to brain in Concord and elsewhere during this era. Whitman's poetry is like Dickinson's, a poetry of the individual, and yet it is clear that Whitman's individual is very different from Dickinson's.

Whitman believed, without doubt, that he was "The Poet" described by and hoped for by Emerson in his essay of the same name. Whitman says as much in the preface to *Leaves of Grass*, his single greatest volume of poetry. While Emily Dickinson may have been willing to remain cloistered and publicly silent in her home in Amherst—as we have seen, her poems were not even known until after her death—Whitman insisted from early on that he was a prophetic, poetic voice of, by and for the "People"—just what Emerson had asked for.

Even Whitman's poetic practice bears comparison with the Transcendentalists. He would write short snippets of his immediate inspiration on slips of printer's paper and these became the "leaves" of *Leaves of Grass*. He collected these lyrics only later and then worked almost throughout his lifetime to organize them into something like a coherent whole. Emerson and Thoreau both visited Whitman in New York, and he came to have a much more public presence than almost any other poet of the 19th century.

There can be no doubt that Whitman saw himself, and then went on to fashion himself, as a version of the figure of "The Poet" that was described by Emerson in his 1844 essay of that title. Emerson had called for a poet who could speak for the people and who would also become a public figure in the life of the nation. In a sense, what Emerson sought to oppose was the romantic idea of the poet, isolated from society. In effect, what Emerson called for was a poet whose artistic vision would be of not only personal use to the poet and to his readers, but would be of public use to the entire nation.

Here was Emerson's lament, quoting from his essay on "The Poet:"

> Our log-rolling, our stumps and their politics, our fisheries, our Negroes, and Indians, our boasts, and our repudiations,

the wrath of rogues, and the pusillanimity of honest men, the northern trade, the southern planting, the western clearing, Oregon, and Texas, are yet unsung.

Here was that sense of Emerson's, that the nation still needed to be sung, and that long list he gives describes those aspects of America that have not yet been given voice.

Whitman echoed almost this identical sentiment by saying in his 1885 preface to *Leaves of Grass* "The United States themselves are essentially the greatest poem." Here is the completion of Emerson's idea; not only is the United States a continental landmass waiting for singers who can sing its glories, according to Whitman, America itself is a sort of poem. Then Whitman goes on to write that poem.

Emerson responded to this first edition of Whitman's poetry—which Whitman had sent to Emerson out of the blue—Emerson responded with a famous letter back to Whitman that was, from that point on, always quoted by Whitman in the preface to subsequent editions of *Leaves of Grass*. Here is how Emerson responded to the volume he had received from Whitman, "I give you joy of your free and brave thought. I have great joy in it. I find incomparable things said incomparably well [...] I greet you at the beginning of a great career."

That wonderful last sentence has become an echoing cry in all Whitman criticism since Emerson penned that line, "I greet you at the beginning of a great career." Clearly, if you are a young poet, that is exactly the sort of comment you want to receive from someone who had the stature of Emerson, as you set out on your literary adventure.

Whitman clearly has precisely the expansiveness and the inclusiveness that appealed to many Transcendentalists. But he also had a practical side that showed that he was not, again, simply the poet isolated from society. His own career as a printer, actually setting type and printing books, was central to his art. In fact, he personally set the type for parts of the first edition of his own works and indeed, the term "grass" was a term that printers use to refer to preliminary or experimental typesetting, what we would call drafts or less than final work. Therefore, "leaves", referring to pages and "grass" referring to these drafts of poems, was the perfect and appropriate title for his volume of writings.

It is also the case that Transcendentalists would have applauded this link between the practical side of life and the more aesthetic, intellectualized poetic aspects of reality, and this open-ended aesthetic. What I mean by that was that Whitman had a willingness to publish what almost amounted to drafts of his work. He revised *Leaves of Grass* on and on, throughout his adult life; he was never quite satisfied with any final version of his work. This idea that the work of art is not a final polished absolute formal masterpiece, but instead records the kind of transience once again, of private experience, that again, moves us away from a more traditional view of poetry toward a much more modern conception.

The Civil War was one of the great shaping influences on a great deal of Whitman's writing and this influence culminated in his elegiac masterpiece, written after the assassination of Abraham Lincoln. That is the poem entitled "When Lilacs Last in the Dooryard Bloom'd." Let me quote a few lines to give a sense both of the new voice that Whitman brings to American poetry, and also of the way he is able to take a public event, an event as profoundly public as the assassination of the President, and render that experience in profoundly personal and emotional terms:

> When lilacs last in the door-yard bloom'd,
> And the great star early droop'd in the western sky in the night,
> I mourn'd—and yet shall mourn with ever-returning spring.
>
> O ever-returning spring! trinity sure to me you bring;
> Lilac blooming perennial, and drooping star in the west,
> And thought of him I love.

We hear in these lines, not only a new voice for poetry, but also language marshaled to new kinds of effects in ways that I will try to explain now. *Leaves of Grass*, as a number of critics have pointed out, brought two important new subjects into American poetry—the importance of sexuality and also the value of human labor, especially physical labor, manual labor. Of course, sex was part of nature, as the more liberal Transcendentalists such as Alcott had taught, and all employment was potentially noble. Traditionally it was only the aristocratic level of work that had been celebrated, especially in verse. For Whitman, all human activity was significant, whether it was the work of the lawyer, the seamstress or the ditch digger, and perhaps most remarkably, in terms of the public response, Whitman was even willing to celebrate the work of the prostitute.

As the contemporary critic, Jerome Loving, has noted in his analysis of Whitman:

> The poet reasoned that if—according to Transcendentalist doctrine—everyone was divine because nature was emblematic of God, then all were equal, politically equal, including women, whom Whitman treated equally with men. ... This idea of equality and self divinity also meant that one could celebrate himself or herself. And so the first poem of the first edition of Leaves of Grass began: 'I celebrate myself, and sing myself, / And what I assume you shall assume, / For every atom belonging to me as good belongs to you.

This is another consistent and repeated conceit within Whitman's poetry—the notion that all of us are connected, both at the level of human equality and almost at the level of physical nature, that my atoms in some sense, connect to your atoms. It is a profoundly material vision at that level, but Whitman consistently extends it into ethical and moral realms. In that sense, Whitman is, above all, our poet of democracy. He takes the idea of democracy, expounded so articulately by the Founding Fathers, and by the middle of the 19th century, he finds a way to apply that democratic ideal to every tier of society, to every member of the human race and to all people, regardless of their background, their color or their occupation.

The sensuousness that I have noted in Whitman caused him problems throughout his career; not only in terms of the direct issue of sexuality, he wrote about the human body however, and about sexual desire in ways that had rarely been attempted and certainly never before in America. Here is a passage from "I Sing the Body Electric:"

> Examine these limbs, red, black, or white—they are so cunning in tendon and nerve;
> They shall be stript, that you may see them.
>
> Exquisite senses, life-lit eyes, pluck, volition,
> Flakes of breast-muscle, pliant back-bone and neck, flesh not flabby, good-sized arms and legs,

And wonders within there yet.

In these remarkable lines we feel Whitman almost peeling back the layers of the body itself to reveal the muscles and the tendons and the sinews beneath and Whitman seems to glory as much in the anatomical details of human anatomy as he does in that perfect Greek image of the exterior of the human body.

As we might imagine with lines like those, Whitman offended many, including many Transcendentalists I am sure, with his open and frank approach to sexuality. Here is how bold Whitman could be, "Have you ever loved the Body of a woman?/Have you ever loved the Body of a Man?

Of course, the second of these questions reminds us that Whitman's own homosexual desire was usually implicit rather than explicit in most of his writing, but it was also evident to many of his readers and it certainly caused people difficulties at that point in the 19th century.

Emerson in fact, tried to present Whitman to the respectable Saturday Club in Boston, but after a group of sexually explicit poems entitled "Enfans d'Adam," or "The Children of Adam", appeared in 1860 in that edition of *Leaves of Grass*, Longfellow, Oliver Wendell Holmes and others, refused to have Whitman admitted to the club.

Later, Emerson, on a famous walk around Boston Common with Whitman, tried to convince the poet to tone down this level of overt sexuality. However, even after the poet refused, Emerson decided that he would remain Whitman's defender. Here is what Whitman said after that famous exchange on Boston Common, as he wrote, "I could never hear the point better put—and then I felt down in my soul the clear and unmistakable conviction to disobey all, and pursue my own way." A very Transcendentalist and also very Whitmanesque notion, "I am going to even disobey Emerson's request. I will pursue my own sense of what is right for me."

Whitman relished the role of the somewhat eccentric outsider, but he also linked that role with not only Emerson's description of the poet, but also with a very American view of the heroic individual. As Emerson had requested, Whitman saw himself as a spokesman for Americans. However, not just for America, but for all of its members, from women to Indians to freed slaves. He clearly knew that some of the positions he was adopting in his writing would set him against culturally accepted ways of thinking and acting, not only in terms of questions about his own personal sexuality, but in terms of his willingness to discuss sexual desire and even his willingness to treat all individuals with such a complete and absolute sense of human equality. Even at a time when society was moving in this direction, Whitman's description of the extent of human equality forced some people to find him too extreme.

Romanticism, as we have seen both in England and in America, had sometimes wanted to depict the poet as an outsider, either too good for society or on the fringes of society. But writers like Wordsworth had already written passionately about the lives of ordinary people and I think this is why Whitman was in trouble with some of his readers. He took even the most ordinary of individuals and elevated them to an almost heroic status in terms of his ability to admire everyone's physical presence, everyone's contribution to the wider society and, as we have suggested, every activity from the life of a senator to the life of a prostitute.

Whitman, in a sense, confronted this own dilemma about the status of individual humans in his famous "Song of Myself," when he says "If you want me again, look for me under your boot-soles." I will read that once more, "If you want me again, look for me under your boot-soles." "Where am I?" says Whitman—this is of course, a beautifully poetic image—"I am here under the soles of your feet. I am as ordinary as the dirt you are walking on, and I am connected to the entire nation as a result."

Of course we need to remember that this is the same poet, in the same poem, who also referred to himself first as "a cosmos," and then as "a loafer." A cosmos, a loafer, the dirt under the soles of your feet; this is clearly a poetry of expansiveness and inclusiveness.

Emerson had also addressed this same problem and solved it in a slightly different way once again, in his essay called "The Poet." Here is how Emerson puts it, "The poet is representative. He stands among partial men for the complete man, and apprises us not of his wealth, but of the commonwealth."

The rest of us are "partial men" according to Emerson; the poet is the "complete man." And what the poet gives us is not only his personal identity, but a sense of our common shared human connection. It will not come as a surprise to imagine that Whitman's life came to be seen as "Romantic" as his art.

He was almost completely self-taught—once again, not unlike Frederick Douglass—after having been apprenticed to a printer at the age of 14. He then went on to have a rough and tumble career as a journalist that certainly helped to prepare him for the kind of poetry that he was going to write. On Long Island he worked first as an innovative school teacher, for the time. Once again, we see the link to education. He actually told his students to call him "Walt," and he often used games to help teach math and spelling at a time when this would have been seen as a very unacceptable method of pedagogy. He traveled widely throughout the North and the South, once again, enhancing his stock of images, and he experienced slavery firsthand when he visited New Orleans.

His lengthy career as a journalist and as an editor included time working for the *Brooklyn Daily Eagle*, then in the south for the *New Orleans Crescent* and finally, after he returned back to Brooklyn, for what was called a "free soil" abolitionist paper.

As I have noted, Emerson and Thoreau, each visited Whitman in New York and they found him to be a unique and remarkable figure. Emerson visited first in 1855, but when the two, Emerson and Whitman, went to Emerson's hotel, the elegant Astor, Whitman's shabby clothes denied him entrance to Emerson's room, the exact same experience that he had at the Saturday Club in Boston.

They met many times during the next three decades and their relationship developed in an interesting way. It seemed always, when we read their exchanges, to mix respect for the other's achievement and intellect with an element of suspicion. It is clear, if we compare Emerson's personality and his public presence to Whitman's, we will understand why there might have been tension there.

Thoreau and Bronson Alcott visited Whitman a year after Emerson had done so. Here is how Alcott described that first meeting between Thoreau and the great poet. Alcott said, "Each man was surveying the other curiously, like two beasts, each wondering what the other would do."

Here we have a surprising image of two figures whose personalities may not have been as distinct as Emerson's and Whitman's. Alcott captures this encounter brilliantly, the two surveying one another, waiting to see how they would respond to this encounter.

Here is how Thoreau went on to describe Whitman shortly after that meeting, and this is an early critique of the poet that captures not only something of Thoreau's personality, but also helps to see some of the tensions in the public reception of Whitman in the 19th century. Here is Thoreau:

> That Walt Whitman, of whom I wrote to you, is the most interesting fact to me at present. [...] There are two or three pieces in the book which are disagreeable, to say the least; simply sensual. [...] But even on this side he has spoken more truth than any American or modern that I know. I have found his poem exhilarating, encouraging [...] On the whole, it sounds to me very brave and American [...] He is awfully good.

Once again, this is the sort of critique that any poet would be happy to hear. What is significant I think is the way Thoreau almost immediately captures the sense of the "exhilarating" energy at the heart of Whitman's voice, but he also senses what he calls a "sensual" quality and some things that Thoreau knows are going to distance Whitman from the general reading public.

By the time of the first unified edition of *Leaves of Grass*, Whitman's unique poetic style was fully formed. His writing was very experimental, he used what we now call the long line in a complete version of free verse—this is not blank verse; remember, blank verse is unrhymed iambic pentameter—Whitman is one of the inventors of free verse, which is to say we can a have a twelve-syllable line, followed by a two-syllable line, followed by a complete sentence, followed by three fragments, followed by any combination of stanzas in any length that seem appropriate. The verse is experimental. It is, for the most part, almost always unrhymed; there is little, if any, consistent meter. In fact, the writing is almost journalistic.

But at the same time, there are moments when Whitman rises to a biblical cadence, where his voice takes on a bardic, prophetic, absolutely, almost religious-sounding tone, and then it turns very quickly to be mundane and ordinary in its description of events in the streets of New York City. In this sense, his voice finally is extremely democratic. I like to think of it as dispersed and dispersing, but also unifying, much like America itself.

We need to remember at this point that one of Whitman's most famous comments from "Song of Myself" is the moment when, knowing he is going to be confronted with this question about why his poetry includes so many details—in fact, including ideas that may seem contradictory—Whitman responds, "Do I contradict myself?/Very well then […] I contradict myself;/I am large […] I contain multitudes;/A foolish consistency is the hobgoblin of little minds."

Before we think of this as a purely egotistical statement on the part of the poet, "I am large, I contain multitudes." "I am allowed to contradict myself," let us remember Emerson, "A foolish consistency is the hobgoblin of little minds." There is an Emersonian idea, transformed into remarkable poetry by Whitman.

Whitman's unconventional style and his substance can be linked to a Romantic, and then to a more specifically American, view not only of poetry, but of the artist himself. This idea of the unconventionality of the artist goes back at least to the Romantics, to figures such as Lord Byron and Percy Shelley, who always existed, in a sense, outside of the accepted conventions of society. But it extends, in the 19th century, to include figures such as Vincent Van Gogh and almost all of the French Symbolists—Baudelaire, Rimbaud, all of these figures whose artistic vision took them outside of accepted standards of social behavior.

This kind of artistic eccentricity, or even excess, has subsequently often been seen as a sign of genius. As we have noted, the artist seems unable to fit into polite society or accepted standards of behavior. We should remember, however, as we connect this idea with Whitman, that the Transcendentalists believe that any idea is worthy of our scrutiny if it is an idea that could possibly lead to a vision of the truth.

With Whitman, as many of those Romantic sensibilities might say, the divine can appear in even the most unlikely places and in that sense, the ordinary can very often be seen as extraordinary. For these reasons, among others, Whitman's influence has extended through many artists and through many ideas.

Ezra Pound, as early as 1915, declared Whitman to be one of the father figures of all of Modernism, and poets from T. S. Eliot to William Carlos Williams to Robert Frost have all agreed with Pound's high praise or they have cited Whitman's direct influence on their writing.

When Allen Ginsberg published his screaming poem, *Howl*, he, as did other Beat poets, delivered what he called the "barbaric yawp." That is a phrase lifted directly from Whitman: "I sound my barbaric yawp over the roofs of the world," from the "Song of Myself." Ginsberg delivered that barbaric yawp directly into the voice of postwar poetry. Even today, we draw a similar link to rock stars or to visual artists whose life and work often pushed them out to the edge of polite society, but who end up reflecting essential aspects of society.

More significant perhaps than the personality of any artist, however, and like so many of the Transcendentalists, Whitman gave voice to early versions of America's gradual progress toward racial, social and sexual freedom.

Now for our final two lectures, we will turn to a summary look at the Transcendentalist effect first on the 19th century.

Lecture Twenty-Three
Transcendentalism's 19th-Century Legacy

Scope:

The significance of Transcendentalism, as we have seen, reached much wider than its impact on literary figures. Ideas about education, many of which influenced public education and experimental forms of private education, helped to change the intellectual lives of many Americans. Educational institutions, while not all equally advanced or revolutionary, tended to move toward the acknowledgment that student-centered education might have advantages over the strict authoritarianism of the past. While votes for women would await the 20th century, the expansion of their rights began in earnest during these years. Periodical journalism underwent important changes because of such publications as *The Dial*, *The Western Messenger*, and *The North Star*. Religious denominations grew, in general, to be more expansive and tolerant. American pragmatism and modern psychology emerged in different ways from a belief in the power of the individual intellect and its connection to a wider social reality. In short, the abstract ideas of Transcendentalism often made their way directly into practical solutions to social problems ranging from religious institutions to school classrooms.

Outline

I. The initial and often-noticed legacy of Transcendentalism was its immediate impact on the liberalization of American theology.

   A. Most Transcendentalists questioned traditional religious dogma and ritual, as well as the details of Christian theology.
      1. They generally accepted the idea that there might be many ways to practice faith, and they especially worried over the fear-based restrictiveness of puritanical Calvinists and conservative Congregationalists.
      2. They argued over specifics but agreed that Christianity wanted reformation.
      3. At one extreme, such thinkers as Emerson and Thoreau left the organized church altogether; at the other, they found their way back to orthodox denominations.

B. There were a number of religious figures we have not discussed in detail, each of whom reminds us of the range and reach of Transcendentalist ideas and actions.

    1. Frederick Henry Hedge (1805–1890) was a Unitarian minister who helped to introduce others to the ideas of Coleridge and German philosophers. For a time, the Transcendentalist Club was known as "Hedge's Club," but by the 1840s, he fell out with members over their increasing liberalism.

    2. Orestes Brownson (1803–1876) was a philosopher and minister who disappointed many of his Unitarian friends when he converted to Catholicism.

    3. Christopher Cranch (1813–1892), like Emerson, left the Unitarian ministry to pursue a career as a poet; when that did not succeed, he became a well-known landscape painter.

    4. George Ripley (1802–1880), founder of Brook Farm, was also a widely respected preacher who refused to believe that heaven and hell were physical locations. His wife, Sarah, described herself as a scientific Deist who believed that Jesus was an outstanding human being but nevertheless just a human.

C. The mood of many at the time suggested that a robust democracy should be able to accommodate these many different religious practices or lack of any practice.

    1. The precise meaning of freedom of religion had not been clearly articulated by the Declaration or the Constitution.

    2. New England had begun as, and remained, the site of more religious experiments than any other region of the United States.

    3. Such theological disagreements were linked to wider social issues, such as slavery, poverty, and women's rights.

    4. The significance of these debates is indicated by the fact that the meanings of Christianity and church-state separation are still hotly debated today.

II. In time, many of the social and educational ideals of the Transcendentalists spread out into wider currents of American thought.

A. The Transcendentalists were a part of the wider American Renaissance, that period from about 1830 to 1880 when the arts flourished in America as never before: literature (the essay, fiction, and poetry), painting, music, sculpture, and architecture.

   1. Even those, such as Melville and Hawthorne, who could not agree with what they saw as the unalloyed optimism of the Transcendentalists, nevertheless responded to the movement and confronted its ideals in their work.

   2. Others, including painters, architects, and designers, while not engaged in the intellectual debates of the movement, still managed to reflect its energy, enthusiasm, and boldness in aspects of 19th-century artistry.

   3. Hudson River landscape painting, for example, embodied a similar attention to naturalistic surroundings and the sublime in nature.

   4. Victorian Gothic architecture, likewise, embodied a link among the craftsman's head, hand, and heart that traces back to A. W. Pugin and John Ruskin in England but also echoed the ideals of Emerson and Thoreau.

B. American journalism owes a similar debt to the group of prolific authors that emerged around Concord and Boston in the 1830s and 1840s.

   1. *The Dial* (1840–1844), the most well known of these periodicals, originated in the Transcendental Club itself, with Margaret Fuller as its first editor, followed by Emerson.

   2. *The Dial* published, for example, Emerson's poetry and prose, Margaret Fuller's "The Great Lawsuit" (later expanded to become *Woman in the Nineteenth Century*), and the earliest published works of Thoreau.

   3. "Ethical Scriptures," a series of translations from the traditions of Asia, appeared once Emerson became the editor (1842).

   4. *The Western Messenger* emerged as a Unitarian monthly in St. Louis in 1835; its goal was to bring the American West to readers in the East and to bring the ideas of New England Transcendentalism to Western readers. Its authors included Emerson, Fuller, Elizabeth Peabody, and Jones Very.

   5. Other important publications of the time included *The Christian Examiner*, the *Boston Quarterly Review*, and *The Atlantic Monthly*, which has published consistently from 1857 to the present day.

   6. Frederick Douglass began publishing *The North Star*, suggesting a beacon, in 1847. Its denunciations of slavery, as well as articles in support of the rights of women and other oppressed peoples, made it the most important abolitionist paper in the years before the war, read by more than 4,000 people in America, the West Indies, and Europe.

   7. In all these cases, periodical journalism became a way of expanding religious and social debate beyond the pulpit and the lecture hall and a way of moving education toward an increasingly mass audience.

C. As we have noted, student-centered educational theories were put into practice.

   1. Children were not seen merely as small adults but as individuals with their own innate ideas.

   2. Learning was an active, engaged process, not the rote memorization of the past. Conversation and discussion were essential to the process.

   3. If the divine could be found in each individual, then freedom of inquiry and action would need to be cultivated in order to reveal it. Education thus had a political dimension as well, because everyone deserved it by natural right.

III. By the end of the 19th century, many of the specific practical experiments of Transcendentalists had ended, but ideas they had promulgated made their way firmly into the American mainstream and various subcultures.

A. Social causes championed by Transcendentalists often succeeded indirectly.

   1. Rights for women, which began during these years, were not completely secured even in the 20th century.

2. The abolition of slavery was complete, but equal rights under law would await the Civil Rights movement of the 1960s and beyond.
3. Poverty, disease, and other forms of social suffering remain on the national agenda to this day, in our own country and around the world.

B. Widespread literacy and public education became goals of the expanding nation.
1. Journalism began to reach a much wider segment of the population.
2. The idea of the popular press became widespread, and the nonfiction essay, especially the nature essay, developed as a uniquely American form.
3. Novels that described (*Margaret: A Tale of the Real and Ideal* by Sylvester Judd, 1851), critiqued (*Moby Dick*, 1851), or satirized (*The Blithedale Romance*, 1852) Transcendentalist concerns eventually led toward increased literary realism and naturalism.
4. American poetry evolved as a more personal and expressive genre under the influence of numerous poets and their imitators: Emerson, Thoreau, Channing, Very, Whitman, Dickinson.
5. Public education began to spread by the 1840s with the rise of property taxes; by the end of the century, it was the expectation of every community.

C. Nineteenth-century materialism gradually overwhelmed the often elusive idealism of these New England thinkers.
1. Industrialism moved many agrarians away from the pastoral possibility, first in the North, even if the pastoral dream had been an illusion. Most people left the farm. Industry then extended to the South soon after the Civil War.
2. Even in literature and the arts, the idealism, philosophical and ethical, of such figures as Thoreau and Emerson gave way to increasing realism and naturalism by the end of the century. Practicality replaced possibility.
3. Unfettered capitalism led to the triumph of numerous robber-barons by the end of the century and prepared the way for the war machines of World War I and beyond.

4. Materialism, both matter and money, became the order of the day by 1900.
5. Transcendentalism lasted as a sort of dream or a set of ideals, but these ideals would go on to have a direct impact on the 20th century, as we shall see in our final lecture.

Essential Reading:

Albanese, Catherine L. *Corresponding Motion: Transcendental Religion and the New America.*

Lopez, Michael. *Emerson and Power: Creative Antagonism in the Nineteenth Century.*

Supplementary Reading:

Cayton, Mary Kupiec. *Emerson's Emergence: Self and Society in the Transformation of New England, 1800–1845.*

Questions to Consider:

1. How were 19th-century political and social movements directly affected by the ideas of the Transcendentalists?
2. The end of slavery, the Civil War, industrialization, women's rights: How might we link each of these historical developments to the ideas of the Transcendentalists?

Lecture Twenty-Three—Transcript
Transcendentalism's 19th-Century Legacy

Now in order to begin our two-part conclusion, we will turn to the question of Transcendentalism's 19th-century legacy. The significance of Transcendentalism, as we have already seen, reached much wider than merely its impact on literary figures. Ideas about education, many of which influenced public education, and experimental forms of private education, helped to change the lives of many Americans. Educational institutions, while not equally advanced or revolutionary, tended to move toward the acknowledgement that various forms of student-centered education might have advantages over the strict authoritarianism of the past.

Likewise, while votes for women would await the 20th century, the expansion of their rights began in earnest during the years we have been discussing. Periodical journalism underwent important changes because of publications by Emerson such as *The Dial* or *The Western Messenger* or *The North Star* by Frederick Douglass. And of course, religious denominations grew in general to be more expansive and perhaps tolerant, at least partly, as a result of the effort of Transcendentalists.

Even American ideas about pragmatism and modern psychology emerged in different ways from beliefs in the power of the individual intellect and that intellect's connection to the wider social reality. In short, what may sometimes look like the abstract ideas of Transcendentalism often made their way directly into practical solutions to social problems, ranging from religious institutions to school classrooms.

Let us look at some specifics. One of the initial, and perhaps most often noted, legacies of Transcendentalism was its immediate and continuing impact on the liberalization of theology in America. Most Transcendentalists, as we have seen, could be identified as individuals who questioned traditional religious dogmas and rituals, as well as the precise details of Christian theology. Whether they retained traces of their Calvinist past or moved almost as far as what we would now see as agnosticism, members of that original Transcendentalist circle all questioned the religion in which they had been raised.

They generally accepted the idea that there might be many different ways to practice religious faith and they especially worried over that fear-based restrictiveness of any form of puritanical Calvinism or of those conservative Congregationalist churches in which so many of them had been raised. They often argued over the specifics of theological questions, but they almost always agreed that Christianity wanted new forms of reformation.

At one extreme—Emerson and Thoreau—they left the organized church altogether; at another extreme, a number of the Transcendentalists found their way back to orthodox denominations or to new versions of traditional denominations.

There were actually a number of important religious figures associated with the Transcendentalist circle that we have not discussed in detail simply because of a lack of time. But each of these individuals, whom I will now describe briefly, reminds us of the range and the reach of transcendental ideas and actions.

Frederick Henry Hedge was a well known Unitarian minister who helped to introduce others to the ideas of Coleridge and to German idealist philosophy. As you may remember, it was actually translations by the poet Coleridge and others that brought many of the important German ideas to an American audience. For a time, in fact, the Transcendentalist Club was actually known as "Hedge's Club," but by the 1840s, Hedge fell out with most of the other members over their increasing liberalism. Almost like a theological denomination, the members of the Transcendentalist group often came together or separated, based on small differences in their specific ideas.

Orestes Brownson was another philosopher and minister who disappointed many of his former Unitarian friends when he converted to Catholicism. Here was a rare case of a Transcendentalist who not only left the traditional denomination of his past, but went to a more traditional, or perhaps more conservative, denomination as he matured.

Another figure, Christopher Cranch, like Emerson, actually left the Unitarian ministry to pursue his career as a poet. When he failed as a poet, he went on to become a well known landscape painter.

George Ripley, whom we have already mentioned as the founder of the Brook Farm community was another widely respected preacher who refused to believe that heaven and hell were physical locations. Even in the middle of the 19th century, if you announced that you did not believe that heaven and hell existed as places where people would actually end up after their death, you could create problems within religious circles. His wife, Sarah, described herself as a scientific deist, a new phrase. She believed that Jesus was an outstanding human being, but was, nevertheless, just a human.

The mood of many people at this time suggested that any robust democracy, especially like the one they wanted for America, should be able to accommodate all of these many different religious practices and perhaps even the lack of any religious practice. Of course, the precise meaning of freedom of religion had never been clearly articulated or defined by either the Declaration of Independence or the United States Constitution. As we know well, we are still debating the actual meaning of freedom of religion, especially the separation of church and state, in our own time.

New England had begun, and also remained, the site of probably more religious experiments than any other region of the United States. I think that is a fair statement to make, based on the fact that so many of the earliest settlers to America had come through the New England ports and especially because so many of the New England colonies had been founded around one or another idea of religious freedom. The way those principles of religious freedom went on to be interpreted determined how specific denominations developed.

As I hope we have seen in this series of lectures, these kinds of theological disagreements were often linked to much wider social issues, such as slavery, poverty and women's rights. The significance of debates such as these were indicated by the fact that the meaning of Christianity and, as I have suggested, of church-state separation are still hotly debated today.

In time, many of the social and educational ideas of the Transcendentalists spread out into wider currents of American thought. As we have seen, the Transcendentalists were part of the wider American Renaissance, that period from about 1830 to roughly 1880, when the arts flourished in the United States as never before. Literature, including the essay, fiction as well as poetry, painting,

©2006 The Teaching Company Limited Partnership

music and even sculpture and architecture all saw a remarkable flowering in the middle of the 19th century, not all of which was connected to Transcendentalism, but I think we can clearly see Transcendentalism and its outgrowths as a subset of some of that same energy.

Even those well known figures such as Hawthorne and Melville, who could not agree with what they often saw as the unalloyed optimism of the Transcendentalists, often responded to the Movement or confronted its ideals in their work, as we have suggested. Others, such as painters, architects and designers, while not engaged in the same intellectual debates that engaged the Movement, still managed to reflect much of its energy, enthusiasm and boldness. For example, Hudson River landscape painting embodied a very similar attention to natural surroundings and to the sublime in nature, so while it would be a mistake to argue that the Hudson River painters were all Transcendentalists, we see a very similar attention to the natural world in their work as we find in Emerson or in Thoreau.

Even Victorian Gothic architecture embodied a crucial link between the craftsman's head, hand and heart that traces back to A. W. Pugin and John Ruskin in England but was clearly echoing the ideas of Emerson and Thoreau.

To turn to another significant subject, American journalism owes a significant debt to that group of prolific authors that emerged around Concord and Boston, especially in the 1830s and 1840s. *The Dial*, which you will remember, was published from 1840 to 1844, was certainly the most well known of the Transcendentalist periodicals. It originated in the early meetings of the Transcendentalist Club itself, with Margaret Fuller as the first editor, followed after two years by Emerson himself. *The Dial* published, for example, much of Emerson's poetry and prose; Margaret Fuller's essay, "The Great Lawsuit," which was later expanded to become her most significant work, *Woman in the Nineteenth Century*; and also the earliest published works of Henry David Thoreau.

"Ethical Scriptures," a series of translations of important works from the traditions of Asia, appeared in *The Dial* once Emerson became the editor in 1842. Once again, we see the influence of traditions, including the Hindu and Buddhist scriptures on the thinking of this group of intellectuals.

Another journal, *The Western Messenger*, emerged as a Unitarian monthly in St. Louis around 1835. Its goal was to bring the American West to readers in the East and to bring the ideas of New England Transcendentalists to Western readers. Its authors, once again, included Emerson, Fuller, Elizabeth Peabody and even Jones Very.

Other important publications around this time included *The Christian Examiner*, *The Boston Quarterly Review* and even *The Atlantic Monthly*, which, as many of you will know, has published consistently from 1857 to the present day. As another part of this flowering of journalism, Frederick Douglass began publishing *The North Star*, suggesting the image of a beacon, in 1847. This journal's denunciations of slavery, as well as articles in support of the rights of women and other oppressed people, made it the most important abolitionist newspaper in the years before the war. It was read by over 4,000 people in America and also in the West Indies and Europe.

In all of these cases, periodical journalism became an important way of expanding religious and social debates beyond the pulpit and the lecture hall and a way of moving education toward an increasingly mass audience. I think, in this respect, it is important for us to recognize that as we have seen in the 19th century, education was not only the province of the home or the classroom, it took place in churches, it took place in public lecture halls and, in fact, we can see a whole series of developments, including the rise of these publications, as linked to the effort to extend certain kinds of knowledge and awareness to an ever larger public. Once again, part of what I have been calling this generalized move toward a democracy that included not only political ideals, but also intellectual life, the arts of the society and a whole series of aspects of human life. Of course, as we have seen in a number of contexts during our lectures, student-centered forms of education were also increasingly put into practice during this era, very often with connections to some of our Transcendentalist figures.

Children, over time, came to be seen not merely as small adults, but as individuals with their own innate ideas, with their own personalities, that needed nurture and sustenance rather than simply to have ideas crammed into their heads. Learning increasingly came to be seen as an active and engaged process, not ideas about rote memorization that had characterized almost all education in the past. And as we have noted, both conversation and discussion became essential to the process. Whenever we walk into a classroom today and see a group of students engaged either in hands-on learning or in forms of discussion amongst themselves or with the teacher, we are really harking back to some of these ideas that originated among Transcendentalist thinkers.

These ideas also connect to the notion that if the divine could be found in each individual, this idea that there is a God in each of us and that the purpose of education is to bring that force of divinity out, then freedom of inquiry and of action would have to be cultivated in order to reveal this part of each personality. Of course, in this sense, education starts to have a political dimension as well, linked to what we would now see as public education since everyone was suddenly seen to deserve this possibility by what the Transcendentalist would have called natural right. Each of us had the right to be able to fulfill our own potential to the greatest extent possible, and if the fulfillment of that potential required certain kinds of education, then it became the obligation of the state to participate in providing that for each of its members.

By the end of the 19th century, it is fair to say that many of the precise practical experiments by this group of Transcendentalists had ended. But that does not mean that ideas they had promulgated did not make their way firmly into the American mainstream and into a variety of subcultures. Those social causes that we saw, championed by the Transcendentalists, often succeeded indirectly or they succeeded more fully over time than they did during the lives of most of the figures we have been discussing.

Rights for women, which certainly began—and were a central topic of discussion—during this era, were not completely secured even in the 20th century. The abolition of slavery may have been complete, but of course, equal rights under the law would have to await the Civil Rights Movement of the 1960s and perhaps even beyond.

If we look at a whole range of issues such as poverty, disease and other forms of social suffering, those questions remain on the national agenda to our own day, in this country as well as around the world. I am not for a moment arguing that the Transcendentalists found ways to solve completely each of the problems they identified, but in a way they focused series of discussions that became central parts of the American dialog as a result of their efforts.

In this sense, widespread literacy and public education became a goal not just of a few individuals, but of almost the entire expanding nation. As we have seen, journalism began to reach a much wider segment of the population and that idea was, of course, linked to increasing literacy in general. The idea of a popular press became widespread and the nonfiction essay, especially what we would now see as the *Nature* essay developed as a uniquely American form. We would not have essayists of the kind we have today without Emerson and Thoreau.

A whole series of novels described, critiqued or satirized Transcendentalists' concerns and those novels eventually led toward increasing realism and naturalism in literature. The descriptive novel I am thinking of would be one such as *Margaret: A Tale of the Real and Ideal* by Sylvester Judd that was published in 1851. The kind of novel that critiqued Transcendentalism, as we have seen, is best embodied in *Moby Dick*, published that same year and the fiction that satirized Transcendentalism, which is most often cited, was Hawthorne's *The Blithedale Romance*, a satire on his time spent at Brook Farm you may remember.

As we have seen in several of our recent lectures, American poetry evolved into a much more personal and much more expressive genre under the influence of a number of poets and their imitators. Emerson, Thoreau, Channing, Very, Whitman and Dickinson all contributed new subject matter to poetry, new voices to poetry or they created poetry that became an important vehicle for the transmission of their own ideas on a wide range of subjects.

Public education in very practical and specific terms began to spread by about the 1840s and 1850s, specifically with the rise of property taxes. The one thing that awaited the full spread of public education was the question about how that would be paid for. That of course, was not a concern that the Transcendentalists spent much time worrying about. But by the end of the 19th century it was clear that the idea of an education, that was the right of every member of society, was also an expectation of almost every community in America. Once public education came into general currency in that way, it was often the ideas of Bronson Alcott or Elizabeth Peabody that found their way into those early public classrooms and, as we have seen, would go on to influence figures such as John Dewey or Maria Montessori.

Nineteen-century materialism ultimately overwhelmed what we would have to see as the sometimes elusive idealism of this group of New England thinkers. When I use the term "materialism" in this context, I am thinking of it in both ways. Philosophical materialism is, you will remember, that idea that all we can ever know about the world is contained in the material objects around us. If we accept that premise, we are inclined toward a much more scientific, much more practical and much more measurable approach to experience. Of course that philosophical principle of materialism shades over into the economic idea of materialism which suggests that people increasingly come to define what is valuable to them in terms of their economic well being. A materialist in this sense is someone who measures success based on material wealth or based on material surroundings. Clearly during the 19th century, both of these kinds of materialism tend to make their way into American society, producing a whole set of surprising results I would have to say, by the beginning of the 20th century.

Industrialism moved many agrarian families away from the pastoral possibility, first in the North, even if some parts of that pastoral dream, as I have argued, were always an illusion. Most people, as we know, leave the farm. They either leave the farm because life on the farm is difficult or they leave because the city offers many more opportunities for material well being. Of course, industry extended into the South not long after the Civil War and by the end of the 19th century, although there was still a widespread agrarian component to society, American culture increasingly started to define itself in terms of the material successes of industrial life and the growth of cities that attracted more and more people.

Even in literature and the arts, the idealism, both philosophical and ethical, of figures such as Thoreau or Emerson starts to give way to increasing realism and naturalism—both terms that start to describe the way artistic representation develops by the end of the 19th century. In this sense I think, practicality, what is reasonable and what is practically possible, starts to replace possibility, starts to substitute for the ideal or the imagined. If we were going to be extreme about this, we might say that unfettered forms of materials capitalism led to the triumph of numerous robber barons by the end of the 19th century and, in perhaps even more insidious ways, started to prepare the way for those war machines of World War I which, as so many historians have suggested, redefined human history forever.

Materialism, both in terms of matter and in terms of money, became the order of the day by 1900. With that slightly pessimistic view, let me suggest now that Transcendentalism, nevertheless, lasted as a set of ideals, perhaps some people would say only as a dream. It is also clear that the ideals we have been examining throughout the course of these lectures—the notion that each person possesses a kind of divinity, the notion that our ability to get in touch with not only our deepest self, but with the truths of the Universe, especially if we are willing to open our mind to the natural world, to those around us and to a whole set of possibilities that perhaps have not even yet been presented to us—that series of ideals still remained in the minds of many people as this more practical vision of society and of reality starts to encroach on people's thinking.

My argument, as you might imagine, is that Transcendentalism lasted not only in this sense of an imagined dream, but in terms of a series of ideals that would have a direct impact on the 20th century and perhaps even beyond, as we will see in our final lecture.

Lecture Twenty-Four
The Legacy in the 20th Century and Beyond

Scope:

Although few, if any, individuals would claim to be Transcendentalists today, the movement has had a direct influence on a wide range of literary, social, and political movements. Mahatma Gandhi and Martin Luther King, Jr., are direct philosophical descendents of Thoreau. Ecumenicism, women's rights, and environmental awareness are modern ways of thinking that owe a direct debt to the remarkable individuals whose lives we have been examining in these lectures. The Unitarian Universalist Church still acknowledges the crucial role played by Transcendentalism in the development of its individualized and humanistic theology. John Dewey and countless other educational reformers have adopted broadly student-centered pedagogies. Like Romanticism in Britain and Germany, Transcendentalism in America was initially a movement of younger people whose ideas were passed on to young and old alike. Although many of its immediately practical ideas were short-lived, its value as an idealistic movement continues even into our own culture. Modern America still owes a great debt to such thinkers as Emerson, Thoreau, Alcott, and Fuller, whose ideas lasted throughout their own lives and beyond.

Outline

I. Central ideas of the New England Transcendentalists have made their way into the modern world.

   A. The Transcendentalist approach to spirituality has been especially important to the development of the Unitarian Universalists and to other liberal ways of thinking.

      1. A sermon entitled "Transcendentalism for a New Age" was delivered at a Unitarian Church in Virginia in 2005.

      2. In it, Jane E. Rosencrans quotes the Emerson scholar David Robinson, who has claimed that Unitarians in America stand "upon the richest theological legacy of any American denomination," even though they do not always recognize this heritage. That legacy is New England Transcendentalism.

3. Likewise, numerous secular, agnostic, and nonreligious Americans draw on ideas first put forth by lecturers and authors in Concord and Boston to support their own modern views of spirituality: the figurative truth of sacred writings, historical approaches to religion, spiritual lives not tied to dogma or traditional ritual.

4. Current emphasis on the practices of Buddhism, Hinduism, and Taoism, like various forms of secular humanism, can be traced back to the method and liberalism of many Transcendentalist thinkers.

B. Emerson is considered by many to be one of the greatest thinkers, if not the most systematic, that America has produced.

1. Philosophers ranging from John Dewey to Stanley Cavell to Richard Rorty have all written or relied on the ideas of Emerson.

2. Dewey called Emerson "the philosopher of democracy."

3. Cavell, in the prestigious Carus Lectures in 1988, said that his goal was "to recommend Emerson, despite all, to the closer attention of the American philosophical community."

4. Rorty, more recently, has lamented the confusing and contradictory aspects of Emerson but adds that Emerson clearly had a powerful and direct influence on thinkers as different as Nietzsche and William James.

5. One strain of modern pragmatism owes its origins to Emerson's willingness to investigate any idea without prejudice or unnecessary reliance on the limitations of earlier ways of thinking.

6. In this sense, he is more important for his method than his conclusion: commitment to the idea of a unifying principle, direct observation, dialogue, and often open-ended conclusion.

C. Thoreau has likewise been quoted and discussed in a wide range of intellectual and literary contexts.

1. When Franklin D. Roosevelt said, "The only thing we have to fear is fear itself," he was almost quoting Thoreau: "Nothing is so much to be feared as fear" (*Journal*, 1851).

2. Gandhi said that Thoreau's "Civil Disobedience" had "left a deep impression" on him.

3. Martin Luther King, Jr., said:

> ...the teachings of Thoreau are alive today, indeed, they are more alive today than ever before. Whether expressed in a sit-in at lunch counters, a freedom ride into Mississippi, a peaceful protest in Albany, Georgia, a bus boycott in Montgomery, Alabama, it is an outgrowth of Thoreau's insistence that evil must be resisted and no moral man can patiently adjust to injustice.

4. The tradition of nonviolent resistance, from Gandhi to King to Lech Walesa, has drawn directly on the powerful argument of the work Thoreau first called "Resistance to Civil Government."

5. Countless contemporary nature writers have cited Thoreau, critiqued Thoreau, or used him as a touchstone for their work: Aldo Leopold, Edward Abbey, Annie Dillard, Barry Lopez, and Terry Tempest Williams, among others.

II. American literature was shaped by and continues to respond to the ideas and spirit of the Transcendentalists.

A. Emerson and Thoreau each brought new voices into American letters.

1. Emerson was seen, then and now, as the prophetic bard of American idealism. His value was his spirit; his limitation, as Thoreau came to see, was his abstractness.

2. Nevertheless, his language was sweeping, swelling, and metaphysical, and it brought something new in its optimistic enthusiasm.

3. Thoreau, meanwhile, brought a meditative, ruminating, more concrete voice into the national literature; he became a spokesperson for nature and for the natural selfhood of each person.

4. Whitman almost invented modern American poetry, partly under the pressure of Emerson's desire for a "Poet" of the entire nation.

B. Even those who had satirized or critiqued the limits of Transcendentalism often did so in recognition of the lasting impact of the movement.

    1. Hawthorne had a close personal relationship with many members, even while he often mocked their impracticality and lack of a sense of evil; he was really an anti-Transcendentalist, a proto-existentialist.

    2. Likewise, Melville simply could not accept the idea that "the universe is benevolent and human nature good" (*The Confidence-Man*). Melville's wild nature is more modern than Wordsworth's, more like Thoreau's on Mount Katahdin: indifferent, unforgiving, ultimately unknowable, like the great white whale, Moby Dick.

    3. Poe, while not as anti-transcendental as Melville, nevertheless depicts a more modern world of spirit than his colleagues in Concord, much darker and more psychological.

C. More recent authors have explored or embodied this debt in poetry, fiction, and the essay.

    1. Poets from Wallace Stevens to Robert Frost voiced this influence and gave it shape in their works.

    2. Emphasis on the value of nonconformity, derived directly from Emerson and Thoreau, plays out in work by F. Scott Fitzgerald, Hemingway, and Faulkner. To conform or not to conform; that becomes the American question.

    3. Thoreau and Emerson, especially, are directly responsible for the modern literary genre know as *ecocriticism*, a mixed genre of interpretation that links writing about place with an understanding of the natural world and an emphasis on ecological awareness.

    4. Emerson is regularly invoked or discussed in recent critical commentary on such living writers as Thomas Pynchon and Jorie Graham.

    5. The nonfiction essay as an American literary genre, as well as the tradition of American nature writing, emerged directly from the authors we have been studying.

III. Often, these ideas are transformed or adapted in important ways.

A. The social and political movements of the 1960s drew strength from ideas related to Transcendentalism even when they did not acknowledge these debts directly.

    1. Race relations in our own era still owe a debt to the abolitionist enthusiasm of Thoreau, Channing, Douglass, and Conway.

    2. Arguments for women's rights trace to Fuller, Peabody, and their supporters, including many men.

    3. Communal living remains an ideal for social movements ranging from hippies to religious cults.

    4. Even current emphasis on globalism links to Transcendentalist ideas about the unity of all people and the value of cross-cultural communication.

    5. The environmental movement, whether it draws on scientific, Native American, Christian, Judaic, or Eastern ways of thinking, links to an anti-materialism at the heart of Transcendentalism.

    6. When people attack the pervasive materialism of our own culture, they often use Thoreau to do so: "A man is rich in proportion to the number of things which he can afford to let alone," and "Money is not required to buy one necessary of the soul" (*Walden*).

B. The institutions they produced may have been short-lived, but their books and ideas are still with us.

    1. Idealism like that of the Transcendentalists is sometimes hard to sustain past youthful enthusiasm, yet today, they continue to inspire young and old alike. As Thoreau said, "In proportion as [a person] simplifies his life, the laws of the universe will appear less complex, and solitude will not be solitude, nor poverty poverty, nor weakness weakness"; or as Emerson noted, "The only reward of virtue is virtue," and "What lies behind us and what lies before us are small matters compared to what lies within us."

    2. The Ralph Waldo Emerson Society was not founded until 1989 as a literary and scholarly site dedicated to the study of the life and work of the "Sage of Concord."

    3. In 1990, rock musician Don Henley of the Eagles began the Walden Woods project, an organization established to preserve Walden Pond and the landscape surrounding it. The Thoreau Institute has now been added as an educational program to assist these efforts; its members include Meryl Streep, Annie Dillard, Michael Douglas, and the rock star Sting.

4. Massachusetts author Jane Langton has described the way these figures still haunt our imaginations:

> Today I can't cross Boston Common without thinking of Emerson walking there with Walt Whitman—nor can I walk up Tremont Street without remembering the Saturday Club at the Parker House. I wish I knew in which Cambridgeport house Emily Dickinson spent many a homesick month while consulting a doctor about her eyes […] Have you ever felt something tickle your cheek as you walk down Brattle Street? I'll tell you what that is—it's the ghostly whiskers of some long-dead transcendentalist.

5. Even a series of lectures like this one links us back to the Transcendentalists' belief in the value of lifelong self-education. The growth of each human mind expands a self-reliant person who is of value to the entire universe.

Essential Reading:

Buell, Lawrence. *The Environmental Imagination: Thoreau, Nature Writing, and the Formation of American Culture.*

Gura, Philip F., and Joel Myerson, eds. *Critical Essays on American Transcendentalism.*

Supplementary Reading:

Rosencrans, Jane E. "Transcendentalism for the New Age." www.vcu.edu/engweb/transcendentalism/ideas/rosecrans.html.

Questions to Consider:

1. Pragmatism, democracy, globalism, environmentalism: How can movements of thought and ideas like these be connected to the influence of Transcendentalism?

2. What would you say is the greatest single impact of Transcendentalism on current ways of thinking in America or around the world?

Lecture Twenty-Four—Transcript
The Legacy in the 20th Century and Beyond

Welcome now to the final lecture in our series on Emerson, Thoreau and the Transcendentalist Movement. In this concluding lecture we will consider the question of Transcendentalism's legacy in the 20th century and even beyond.

Although few, if any, individuals would now claim to be Transcendentalists, the Movement has clearly had a direct influence on a wide range of literary, social and even political movements. Mahatma Gandhi and Martin Luther King, Jr. have both said that they are direct descendents of Thoreau. Ecumenicism—that is the tendency to bring different religions and different denominations within religions into productive dialog—as well as women's rights and even environmental awareness are all modern ways of thinking that owe a direct debt to that remarkable group of individuals whose lives we have been examining in these lectures. For example, the Unitarian Universalist Church still acknowledges a crucial role played by Transcendentalism in the development of its individualized and humanistic theology. John Dewey and countless other educational reformers have adopted broadly student-centered pedagogies, such as those we saw pioneered by Bronson Alcott and Elizabeth Peabody.

As the movement of Romanticism in Britain and in Germany earlier in the 19th century, Transcendentalism in America was initially a Movement of primarily younger people whose ideas were then passed on to young and old alike. Although many of its immediately practical suggestions were short lived, its value as an idealistic movement continues even into our own culture, in way that I will explore. Modern America still owes a direct debt to the ideas of thinkers such as Emerson, Thoreau, Alcott and Fuller; all of whose ideas lasted throughout their own lives and beyond.

Central principles advocated by the New England Transcendentalists have clearly made their way directly into our modern world. The Transcendentalist approach to spirituality for example, has been especially important to the development of the Unitarian Universalist denomination and to other liberal ways of thinking about religious truth. A sermon entitled "Transcendentalism for a New Age", in fact, was delivered in 2005 at a Unitarian parish in Virginia. In that sermon, Jane E. Rosecrans quotes the Emerson scholar, David Robinson, who claimed that Unitarians in America, in his words, stand "upon the richest theological legacy of any American denomination," even though the members of those parishes do not always recognize this heritage. The legacy that Robinson had in mind was that of New England Transcendentalism.

Likewise, a number of secular, agnostic and even nonreligious Americans continued to draw on ideas that were first put forth by those lecturers and authors in Concord and Boston to support their own more modern views of spirituality. By this I mean, for example, the figurative truth of sacred writings, the idea that a sacred scripture does not always have to embody only literal facts or historical events, but a more historicized approach to religion that tries to see religious history and religious denominations as partly the function of real human beings living during actual historical times with their own unique sets of circumstances.

And finally, many modern individuals have tried and continued to work to develop spiritual lives that are not always tied to individual dogmas or to traditional rituals. Current emphasis on the practice of Buddhism, Hinduism or Taoism, and a number of forms of completely secular humanism, can be linked to the method and to the general liberal mode of inquiry that was practiced by so many of the Transcendentalist thinkers.

Emerson is to this day, considered by many to be one of the greatest, if not perhaps always the most systematic, of the thinkers that America has produced. Important philosophers ranging from John Dewey to Stanley Cavell and Richard Rorty have all written on, or have relied on, the ideas of Emerson, either in their own works or in discussing the important influences of the history of philosophy on their own ideas. Indeed, John Dewey called Emerson "the philosopher of democracy," a point that we have tried to make repeatedly in these lectures that suggests how the political notion of democracy established and put forth by the Founding Fathers of America was taken up by a thinker such as Emerson and applied to a whole range of philosophical, intellectual and social concerns. The idea that what a democracy would really require was well educated, equal individuals, all of whom would have a shared stake in the good of the republic and all of whom would be in a position to exercise those votes that they were granted by the Constitution.

Stanley Cavell, in delivering the prestigious Carus Lectures in 1988, said that his own goal was "to recommend Emerson, despite all, to the closer attention of the American philosophical community." What Cavell seems to have meant in that "despite all" phrase is that Emerson, in his view, has not always been taken as seriously, especially by academic philosophy, as he perhaps warrants and this perhaps links to the idea about Emerson's abstract ways of thinking and the fact that, clearly, he presented not a unified system but a cluster of related philosophical ideas.

Richard Rorty—more recently, one of the founders of what has come to be called "Neo-Pragmatism" or a new version of pragmatism—Rorty has lamented what we have seen and discussed and the confusing and contradictory aspects of Emerson's thought. But Rorty has added that Emerson also had a powerful and significant influence on thinkers as different and as significant as Nietzsche and William James.

I think it goes without saying that one strain of modern pragmatism—the notion of linking philosophical ideas to the immediately practical, to how those ideas will actually play out in personal lives or in social circumstances—one strain of that kind of pragmatism owes at least part of its origins to Emerson's willingness to investigate almost any idea without prejudice or perhaps more important, without unnecessary reliance on the limitations of earlier ways of thinking. Emerson was constantly reminding his listeners and his readers that in many instances it was the idea of the past that held us back from the obvious truths that we could see around us in our own immediate experience of the natural world, in our own interaction with our families and the groups of individuals to whom we were closest and even in our relationship to the wider state.

In this sense I think, in this concluding lecture, it is important to remember that Emerson may prove, over time, more important for his methods than for any specific conclusion he reaches. His commitment to the idea of a unifying principle that may help us hold together whichever set of concerns we are addressing in an individual instance. His emphasis on the value of direct observation on the use of our own sensuous awareness to give us a picture of the world that helps tell us something, in Emerson's sense, about what may transcend that world, about what lies beyond that world and often his repeated emphasis on dialog and the often open-ended conclusion, the idea that we need not always reach a syllogistic logically absolute conclusion to any problem, but that we can come up with either a series of alternate solutions or an acceptance of the need for ongoing dialog and conversation.

Of course Thoreau has likewise been quoted and discussed in perhaps even a wider range of intellectual and literary contexts, especially in recent years. When Franklin D. Roosevelt said that "The only thing we have to fear is fear itself," he was almost quoting Thoreau. Many people are surprised to learn that in his *Journal* in 1851, Thoreau had written "Nothing is so much to be feared as fear." I am not arguing here necessarily that Roosevelt took his quotation directly from Thoreau—that is always hard to know in a historical sense—what I am suggesting is that modern thinkers have very often tapped into or drawn on very similar sorts of observations.

In a more specific way, Mahatma Gandhi in India said that Thoreau's "Civil Disobedience" had left what he called "a deep impression" on him. You will remember that we have already noted that Gandhi actually read selections from that essay that we have come to call "Civil Disobedience," to hundreds of thousands of Indian people bent on democracy and setting out to achieve their own independence from British Colonial Rule. Here, in the modern world, we see a direct application of Thoreau's philosophical principle about the need and the value of breaking unjust societal laws applied to a continent and to a people that were halfway around the world.

Martin Luther King, Jr. was approached in the 1960s to submit information for a magazine article about those thinkers who had been influential on the development of his own ideas, especially those that were directly connected the Civil Rights Movement and here is what King said:

> ...the teachings of Thoreau are alive today, indeed, they are more alive today than ever before. Whether expressed in a sit-in at lunch counters, a freedom ride into Mississippi, a peaceful protest in Albany, Georgia, a bus boycott in Montgomery, Alabama, it is an outgrowth of Thoreau's insistence that evil must be resisted and no moral man can patiently adjust to injustice.

There is a wonderful phrase out of King's mouth, "no moral man can patiently adjust to injustice." Once again, we see how King, bent on a very specific mission, that of applying his principles of civil rights to the circumstances in America in the 1950s and 1960s, once again, draws directly on Thoreau and says that Thoreau's ideas are not merely abstract idealized principles, they are actually occurring, as he points out, at lunch counters, on freedom rides and even in boycotts in Alabama.

Indeed the much more general tradition that we have come to see as nonviolent resistance, perhaps not always as fully nonviolent as we would wish—but we should remember now that in a careful examination of Thoreau, we saw that his message was not always strict nonviolence, it was about the importance of being civilly disobedient at times when the state had produced laws that did not correspond to ones own innate sense of morality. That tradition extends from Gandhi and from King to Lech Walesa in Poland and it has drawn directly on the powerful argument of the work that Thoreau first called "Resistance to Civil Government." I think, once again, we should keep that notion of resistance in mind as we remember his important essay.

Countless contemporary nature writers have cited Thoreau, have critiqued Thoreau or have used him as touchstones for their own work. I am thinking about a group of writers that would include Aldo Leopold, Edward Abbey, Annie Dillard, Barry Lopez and Terry Tempest Williams, among many others. These are writers who all either quote Thoreau directly, suggest his influence on their own thoughts about the natural world and the way they have come to describe that world.

American literature, as we have seen in details, was shaped by, and continues to respond in interesting ways, to the ideas and also to the spirit of those New England Transcendentalists. Emerson and Thoreau each brought a new voice directly into American letters. Emerson was seen, both then and now, as the almost prophetic bard of American idealism. He value, as I have tried to suggest, was often his spirit, his enthusiasm and especially the impassioned effective rhetoric with which he was able to deliver his ideas. His limitation, as Thoreau came to see, among many others, was often his abstractness. Nevertheless, Emerson's language was sweeping, swelling, metaphysical and I think it brought something new in its optimistic enthusiasm to the spirit that began to pervade America. America, in its early years, was clearly seen as a land of promise and a land of challenge. By the time of Emerson, we start to have the feeling that anything may be possible in America. Even if that is still considered too idealistic a position to occupy, that spirit has remained in a great deal of American writing.

Thoreau meanwhile, brought what I would call a meditative, ruminating and a much more concrete voice into our national literature. He became a spokesperson for nature, but perhaps more important, for the natural selfhood of each person. Thoreau's purpose, as we have suggested, was not simply to encourage us all to retreat to a small cabin in the woods; Thoreau wanted us to implant that idea of Walden in our own minds and carry it with us, whether we were in Manhattan or Los Angeles.

As a result of these influences, a figure such as Walt Whitman almost reinvented American poetry, partly as we have seen, under that pressure of Emerson's desire for a "Poet" with a capital "P", a new kind of poet who could serve not just his own ideas of those of an elite group of readers, but could in some sense be a "Poet" for the entire nation.

Even those who satirized or critiqued the limits of Transcendentalism often did so in recognition of the power that became part of its lasting impact. Let me give several examples. Nathaniel Hawthorne, as we have noted, had a close personal relationship with many members of the Transcendentalist circle even while he often mocked their impracticality and their lack of a sense of evil. In some ways Hawthorne was almost an anti-Transcendentalist. I like to think of him as a proto-existentialist; what I mean by that is he was never convinced by their thorough-going optimism in a principle of goodness that lay just behind the bounds of our perception. Hawthorne always retained that New England puritan sense that there was evil lurking just beyond us and that perhaps our own psyches were tainted in a way that we could never fully escape.

In a similar, but also significantly different way, Melville could not accept the idea, as he put in his work, *The Confidence-Man*, that "the Universe is benevolent and human nature good." In this sense of course, his figure, Ahab, finds it impossible to imagine a Universe that is pervaded by the kinds of optimism that people associated with

Emerson or even a wild nature that was as positive as Thoreau's. In fact, Melville's view of nature comes close to Thoreau's in that remarkable passage on Mount Katahdin in Maine, a nature that is indifferent, unforgiving, and ultimately unknowable, not unlike the great white whale, Moby Dick.

Edgar Allan Poe, while perhaps not as anti-Transcendental as either Hawthorne or Melville, nevertheless, depicts a more modern world of spirit than his colleagues in Concord. I think the simplest thing to say is that Poe's world of spirit is much darker and more psychological, as we would now say.

More recent authors have explored or embodied their debt to the Transcendentalists in poetry, in prose fiction and in the essay. Poets from Wallace Stevens to Robert Frost have voiced this influence and given it shape in their works. Emphasis on the value of a certain kind of nonconformity comes out of Emerson and Thoreau and then plays out in complicated ways, in works by F. Scott Fitzgerald, Hemingway and even Faulkner. To conform or not to conform, that is a question that the Transcendentalists posed to us and it remains an important American question.

Thoreau and Emerson especially, are directly responsible for almost a new literally genre, now known as ecocriticism. That is a mixed genre of literary and natural interpretation that links any writing about places with an understanding of the realities of the natural world and what we would now see as an emphasis on ecological awareness; that is an appreciation of the connections that hold all the parts of the natural world in unity.

Emerson is even invoked and discussed in very recent critical commentary about a surprising range of living writers that include everyone from the experimental novelist, Thomas Pynchon, to the remarkable poet, Jorie Graham. In fact, the nonfiction essay, as an American literary genre, as well as the growing body and tradition of American nature writing, emerge almost directly from this group of writers we have been studying. It is also important to realize in any sort of a concluding lecture that these ideas have been transformed and adapted in important ways, and that is the question to which I would like to turn now.

The social and political movements of the 1960s and beyond drew a great deal of strength from ideas that were related to

Transcendentalism, even when they did not acknowledge these debts directly. Race relations, even into our own era, in the 21st century, still owe a debt to the abolitionist enthusiasm of Thoreau or Channing, Frederick Douglass or Moncure Conway. Arguments for women's rights in discussions that we are still having, from classrooms to the Congress of the United States, trace back to Fuller, Elizabeth Peabody and their supporters, including we should remember, many men.

Even communal living remains an ideal for social movements that in our own era range from hippies to a variety of religious cults and other groups who have asked if there are new ways to organize family and social life.

Our current emphasis on globalism, on the relationships of the United States to other countries, finally can be linked to certain Transcendentalist ideas about the unity of all people, regardless of race, regardless of their country of origin and about the value of what we would not call cross-cultural communication. When Emerson and Moncure Conway traveled to England for example, they carried ideas from the Transcendentalists with them and we have seen a fruitful interplay between Europe and America moving in both directions throughout these lectures.

The environmental movement, whether it draws on scientific, Native American, Christian, Judaic or even Eastern ways of thinking, links to anti-materialism—to an emphasis that draws us away from the urban industrialism of the last century and a half that is at the heart of Transcendentalism, a view that there is something in the natural world distinct from society that can still offer something that we all need.

When people attack the pervasive materialism of our own culture, they often still use Thoreau to do so. Let me give just two quick examples: "A man is rich in proportion to the number of things which he can afford to let alone," very important that Thoreau uses the word "afford" at the end of that statement in order to remind us that richness has nothing to do with what we can afford in a material sense. Later Thoreau says "Money is not required to buy one necessary of the soul." Thoreau is adamant about this throughout all of his writing. If we want to know what is necessary, the last place we look is our wallets.

The institutions the Transcendentalists produced may have been short lived in practical terms, but their books and their ideas are still with us in important and significant ways. It is clear that idealism such as theirs is sometimes hard to sustain past our own youthful enthusiasm, and yet today, I do think many of the Transcendentalists continue to inspire both young people and older people alike. As Thoreau said once again, "In proportion as a person simplifies his life, the laws of the universe will appear less complex and solitude will not be solitude, nor poverty poverty, nor weakness weakness." Here, in a single sentence, Thoreau gives us a means to eradicate solitude, poverty and weakness; and the answer, according to Thoreau, is simplifying our life, the point at which even the laws of the Universe will turn out to be simple.

Emerson makes two related claims, 'The only reward of virtue is virtue; we can't be seeking the good for anything but the good's own reward." And then, "What lies behind us and what lies before us are small matters compared to what lies within us." That is a wonderful passage toward the end of this series of lectures.

The Ralph Waldo Emerson Society, we may be surprised to learn, was not founded until 1989, but it is still an active and engaged literary and scholarly society, dedicated to the study of the life and the work of that great Sage of Concord.

In 1990, the rock musician Don Henley, of a band called the Eagles, began what he described as the "Walden Woods Project." This was an organization established and dedicated to the preservation of Walden Pond itself, the physical pond, and to the landscape surrounding it. The Thoreau Institute has now been added as an education program for this project to assist in these efforts. The members of that group include the actress Meryl Streep; the nature writer Annie Dillard; the actor Michael Douglas; and even the rock star Sting.

Finally, let me give you a quote from Massachusetts author, Jane Langton, in which she describes the way these Transcendentalist figures may still haunt our imaginations. Here is what Langton has to say:

> Today I can't cross Boston Common without thinking of Emerson walking there with Walt Whitman—nor can I walk up Tremont Street without remembering the Saturday Club

at the Parker House. I wish I knew in which Cambridgeport house Emily Dickinson spent many a homesick month while consulting a doctor about her eyes […] Have you ever felt something tickle your cheek as you walk down Brattle Street? I'll tell you what that is—it's the ghostly whiskers of some long-dead transcendentalist.

For Jane Langton, they are still here; all we need to do is associate ourselves with their memory.

And, of course, by way of final conclusion, let me remind us that even a series such as the one we have just completed links us back to a Transcendentalist belief in the value of lifelong self-education. The growth of each human mind expands a self-reliant person who is of value to the entire Universe.

Timeline

1780 ....William Ellery Channing born in Newport, Rhode Island (died 1842).

1798 ....William Wordsworth and Samuel Taylor Coleridge, *Lyrical Ballads.*

1799 ....Amos Bronson Alcott born (died 1888); Rosetta Stone discovered in Egypt.

1802 ....William Paley, *Natural Theology: or, Evidences of the Existence and Attributes of the Deity, Collected from the Appearances of Nature.*

1803 ....Ralph Waldo Emerson born in Boston (died 1882).

1804 ....Elizabeth Palmer Peabody born in Massachusetts (died 1894).

1807 ....Lord Byron, *Hours of Idleness*; Wordsworth "Ode: Intimations of Immortality."

1810 ....Margaret Fuller (died 1850) and Theodore Parker (died 1860) both born in Massachusetts.

1817 ....Henry David Thoreau born in Concord (died 1862).

1818 ....Byron, *Don Juan*; Keats, *Endymion*; Mary Wollstonecraft Shelley, *Frankenstein.*

1819 ....William Ellery Channing preaches "Unitarian Christianity"; Walt Whitman born on Long Island (died 1892).

1830 ....Emily Dickinson born in Amherst, Massachusetts (died 1886); Charles Lyell, *Principles of Geology.*

1832	Elizabeth Palmer Peabody publishes *First Steps to the Study of History*; Emerson preaches the "Lord's Supper" sermon and resigns his pastorate.
1834	Charles Babbage invents first computer ("analytical engine"), assisted by Byron's daughter, Ada Lovelace.
1835	Wordsworth, *Poems*; *Record of a School* published anonymously by Elizabeth Palmer Peabody about Bronson Alcott's Temple School.
1836	Transcendental Club formed; Emerson's *Nature* published anonymously.
1837	Emerson delivers "The American Scholar" address at Harvard.
1838	Emerson's "Divinity School Address"; Frederick Douglass escapes from slavery.
1839	Elizabeth Palmer Peabody opens West Street Bookstore.
1840	*The Dial* magazine begins publication, lasting until 1844.
1841	Brook Farm founded; Emerson's *Essays: First Series* published.
1842	Emerson's son Waldo dies, "Threnody"; William Ellery Channing dies.
1844	Robert Chambers, *Vestiges of the Natural History of Creation*.
1845	Margaret Fuller publishes *Woman in the Nineteenth Century*; Thoreau at Walden.

1846	Thoreau jailed for failure to pay tax; Emerson's poems published.
1847	Thoreau leaves Walden; Margaret Fuller settles in Italy.
1849	Thoreau publishes "Resistance to Civil Government," later called "Civil Disobedience."
1850	Margaret Fuller, her husband, and their son, Angelo, drown off Fire Island, New York; her manuscript history of the Italian revolution is lost; Tennyson, *In Memoriam*; Wordsworth dies.
1851	Herman Melville, *Moby Dick* (based on the sinking of the whale-ship *Essex* in 1820).
1854	Thoreau, *Walden; Or, Life in the Woods* published; Anthony Burns convicted of being a fugitive slave; 50,000 in Boston watch him taken in shackles to a ship; Henry David Thoreau delivers his address known as "Slavery in Massachusetts" in Framingham; Emerson and Thoreau meet Walt Whitman.
1855	Walt Whitman's *Leaves of Grass* published; Herbert Spencer, *Principles of Psychology*.
1859	John Brown leads a raid on the armory at Harpers Ferry; hanged in Charles Town (now West Virginia); Henry David Thoreau delivers "A Plea for Captain John Brown" in Concord; Elizabeth Palmer Peabody develops interest in kindergartens; Darwin publishes *On the Origin of Species by Means of Natural*

Selection, which concludes "There is grandeur in this view of life."

1862 ....Julia Ward Howe publishes "Battle Hymn of the Republic" in *The Atlantic Monthly* after visiting an army camp near Washington, D.C.; Thoreau dies.

1880 ....Elizabeth Palmer Peabody publishes *Reminiscences of Rev. Wm. Ellery Channing*.

1882 ....Emerson dies and is buried in Sleepy Hollow Cemetery, Concord.

Glossary

Abolitionist: A person who is strongly committed to the unjustness of and need to end human slavery, generally by nonviolent means, although sometimes resorting to violence.

American Renaissance: A movement in the arts and society, from roughly 1830–1880, which saw a flowering of creative activity throughout the country. Melville, Whitman, Hawthorne, Poe, Stowe, Thoreau, and Emerson are all considered representative of the period, but the phrase also refers to important developments in the visual arts and architecture up to the end of the 19th century.

Calvinism: A set of theological beliefs and practices deriving from the life and teachings of John Calvin. Calvinists emphasize predestination, the omnipotent power of God, salvation by grace, and the sinfulness of mankind.

Congregationalist: Any one of a number of churches that based their governance solely around each congregation; not so much a specific denomination as a way of describing the organizational structure of the church.

The Dial: A magazine that was the first formal publication of the Transcendentalist Club (1840–1844), edited first by Margaret Fuller and later by Emerson; it later reappeared as an important literary magazine of the Modernists, edited by Marianne Moore from 1925–1929.

Fugitive Slave Act: A law passed by Congress in 1850 that made it illegal for law enforcement officials to fail to arrest runaway slaves. The act became a rallying cry for abolitionists and led to greatly increased activity on the Underground Railroad.

German Idealism: A school of philosophy deriving primarily from Immanuel Kant's response to the skeptical materialism of David Hume. The movement became linked to Romanticism and to revolutionary political ideas. Its leading practitioners included Johann Gottlieb Fichte, Friedrich Schelling, and Georg Wilhelm Friedrich Hegel. In literature, this form of idealism is often connected to Goethe.

Higher criticism: A movement, primarily in Germany and England, that argued that religions should be studied from a historical perspective and that the Bible and the life of Jesus needed to be examined as historical events. Higher critics sought to interpret the Bible as a literary work and to investigate its claims objectively or scientifically.

Idealism: The philosophical position that gives ideas supremacy over material things. Philosophical idealism sees the mind, the spirit, and the realm of ideas as fundamental; ethical idealism places moral values above all others.

Immanence: In theology, the belief that the divine is contained within reality, either in the totality of reality or in some significant portion. An immanent God can be found within people, places, or things; a transcendent God lies somehow above or beyond us and our sensory perceptions. This distinction became important to 19th-century liberal theology.

Individualism: A view that emphasizes the importance of individuals over societal groups and stresses human freedom and the role of the individual in determining moral value. A specifically naturalistic version of individualism in the minds of many Transcendentalists suggested that individuals could find many of the truths they needed in the natural world.

Materialism: In philosophy, the idea that matter is all that finally exists or that material substance comprises the fundamental reality. In social discourse, materialism suggests overemphasis on the value of wealth and material objects.

Mythology: The body of stories, ideas, and beliefs produced, usually by primitive cultures, to explain inexplicable aspects of nature or human life. Mythology stresses the symbolic aspect of reality through which one thing can stand in for another.

Natural theology: The belief that characteristics of divinity can be perceived within or through the natural world. Negative aspects of nature—death, disease, destruction—pose particular problems for this view of divinity.

Noumena: A term coined by the philosopher Immanuel Kant to describe the unknowable aspect of reality which nevertheless provides the basis for all that we can understand. In Kant's system, the human mind provides innate concepts (like space and time) through which noumena appear to us as sensory phenomena—the objects and events around us.

Pantheism: The theological belief that God resides in everything, sometimes identified mistakenly with paganism, although many pagan religions are pantheistic.

Pragmatism: The idea that the standard for value is usefulness. A pragmatist believes, broadly, that ideas that lead to useful, practical results are good ideas. Pragmatists tend to prefer applied ethical rules—which produce positive results in specific cases—to abstract ethical concepts.

Puritanism: The body of beliefs that grew up around a group of radical Protestant reformers in England after the Reformation. Puritans were, for the most part, Calvinists who emphasized austere ways of life and strict adherence to religious rules.

Romanticism: The broad cultural movement that arose, especially in Germany and England, at the close of the 18th century and into the early 19th century. Romantics emphasized the value of emotions, the importance of human connections to the natural world, and a willingness to question all forms of social, political, and religious authority. American Romanticism emerged slightly later and overlapped in important ways with Transcendentalism and the American Renaissance.

Scientific rationalism: The belief that the only valid form of knowledge is produced by science—direct observation of physical phenomena—combined with the operations of the rational mind. On this view, such categories as human emotions or aesthetics (judgments about beauty) have no use, because they are based on subjective claims that can never be verified. Likewise, spirituality is a meaningless realm for scientific rationalists, because spiritual claims are based on subjective beliefs that can never be observed or measured.

Transcendentalism: A term derived from the "transcendental" philosophy of Immanuel Kant that characterizes a broadly related cluster of ideas that emerged as a part of the American Renaissance. Proponents of this way of thinking emphasized the divine in nature, the value of the individual and of human intuition, and an ideal spiritual reality that "transcends" sensory experience and provides a better guide for life than narrowly empirical or logical reasoning.

The term refers to a cluster of concepts set forth by a number of individuals, rather than a fixed or formal philosophy.

Unitarianism: A liberal religious denomination that emerged out of Congregationalist churches in New England in response to the strict Calvinism of the Puritan settlers. Joseph Priestley was instrumental in bringing Unitarianism to America from England. Unitarians argued against the idea of the Trinity, and they became a more liberal denomination as the 19th century progressed.

Utopia: Literally "nowhere." The idea of a perfect society, sometimes imagined as achievable on Earth, more often seen as purely literary or fantastic. Ideas of utopias range from the Garden of Eden to Star Trek.

Biographical Notes

Alcott, Amos Bronson (1799–1888). The father of Louisa May Alcott, A. Bronson Alcott was one of the foremost Transcendentalists in the years leading up to the Civil War. Alcott was best known in his own era as an educator and as founder of the Temple School and the short-lived Fruitlands community.

Alcott, Louisa May (1832–1888). The daughter of A. Bronson Alcott, Louisa May went on to become more famous than her father as the author of *Little Women* and other widely read novels. Although now considered a children's author, in her lifetime, Alcott wrote works for adults and was an active abolitionist and supporter of women's rights.

Brown, John (1800–1859). An abolitionist and social reformer, Brown's violent methods emerged in Bleeding Kansas and culminated in the raid on Harpers Ferry. Brown's execution by hanging led him to be seen as a lunatic traitor by some and as an abolitionist martyr by others.

Carlyle, Thomas (1795–1881). Carlyle was an English author and social critic who had a powerful impact on the founders of New England Transcendentalism. Carlyle's *Sartor Resartus* advocated a secular spirituality and his *On Heroes and Hero Worship* set forth the idea of the importance of powerful personalities to history.

Channing, William Ellery (1780–1842). Dr. Channing, as he came to be known, was an honorary founder of New England Transcendentalism. A Unitarian minister who became widely influential for his liberal theology and his social activism, he was a moderate thinker who disagreed with all forms of extremism.

Channing, W. Ellery (1817–1901). The younger Channing was the eccentric nephew of the more famous Dr. Channing. Ellery (as he came to be known) had close connections to Emerson and, especially, Thoreau. Emerson published his abstract poems, and Channing visited Thoreau at Walden often, later writing the first biography of his friend.

Coleridge, Samuel Taylor (1772–1834). An English poet and philosopher who, along with Wordsworth, was one of the first-generation founders of British Romanticism; Coleridge's ideas were extremely important to Transcendentalist thinkers. His idealism emphasized a link between the material and the spiritual realms, and he distinguished between our understanding, which results from rational thinking, and our reason, a higher form of thinking that puts us in touch, via intuition, with a realm of pure ideas.

Conway, Moncure (1832–1907). Conway was a Unitarian preacher and, later, a lecturer who eventually left his denomination over his increasingly humanistic thinking. He was one of the few Transcendentalists who came from the American South, and he eventually moved to England, where his freethinking ideas were more widely accepted than anywhere in America.

Dickinson, Emily (1830–1886). She was the reclusive poet of Amherst, Massachusetts, who penned roughly 1,800 lyrics, almost all of which are distinguished by remarkable uses of language, but only a handful of which were published during her lifetime. Known for the dense and psychologically astute content of her poems, she has become a subject of intense biographical speculation in recent years.

Douglass, Frederick (1818–1895). A former slave, he was an abolitionist and reformer who advocated a transformation of America's racial and social ideals. Douglass was best known in his lifetime for the power of his oratory and the impact of his autobiographical writings. He advised Abraham Lincoln during the Civil War and attended the first women's rights convention in Seneca Falls, New York.

Emerson, Ralph Waldo (1803–1882). Seen by many as the philosophical founder of New England Transcendentalism, Emerson was surely its most influential spokesperson and a thinker who had a widespread impact on 19th-century culture. Emerson broke with the organized church early in adult life. He went on to use his oratory and essays to advocate a wide range of ideas about "Nature," "Self-Reliance," "The American Scholar," "The Over-Soul," and "The Poet," ideas that have helped to shape theological, social, and literary developments to the present day.

Fuller, Margaret (1810–1850). The most influential of the female Transcendentalists, Fuller was the first editor of the journal *The Dial* and the author of *Woman in the Nineteenth Century*. She served as one of the first female journalists and foreign correspondents, working for Horace Greeley's *New York Tribune*. After living in Europe for a number of years, she died tragically by drowning, along with her husband and son, in sight of Fire Island.

Hawthorne, Nathaniel (1804–1864). Perhaps best described as an anti-Transcendentalist, Hawthorne found ideas like those of Emerson far too optimistic for his liking. Hawthorne nevertheless lived in one of the Emerson family houses in Concord, married the sister of Elizabeth Peabody, and spent time on the Brook Farm community, which he satirized in *The Blithedale Romance*.

Kant, Immanuel (1724–1804). Kant was a German philosopher who advocated a middle ground between the pure idealism of Plato and the reductive empiricism of Locke. According to Kant, we can know the phenomena that surround us via our senses, but we can never know the underlying *noumena* on which phenomena are based. Kant's version of such a mediated idealism became the basis of Emerson's philosophy and subsequently crucial for many American Transcendentalists.

Melville, Herman (1819–1891). An American author who dealt with Transcendentalist thinking in his masterpiece, *Moby Dick*, Melville also satirized Transcendentalists, especially Emerson, for what he took to be their overly optimistic outlook. Melville is a key figure in the American Renaissance, and his literary works, including such masterpieces as *Billy Budd*, *The Confidence-Man*, and *Typee*, have had a powerful influence on subsequent fiction.

Parker, Theodore (1810–60). Parker was a liberal Unitarian whose hostility to the idea of miracles, and whose emphasis on the historical basis of all religious truth, caused many people to break with his humanistic outlook. He spoke out powerfully in favor of women's rights and the abolition of slavery, and he came to see his ministry primarily as a way of striving to bring about social justice.

Peabody, Elizabeth Palmer (1804–1894). She was an educational reformer and an associate of many members of the Transcendentalist circle. Along with her less famous sisters, Sophia (1809–1871), an artist who married Nathaniel Hawthorne, and Mary (1807–1887), one of the cofounders with her eldest sister of the kindergarten movement in America, Elizabeth became one of the most influential women of her era.

Pestalozzi, Johann H. (1746–1827). The most well-known European educational reformer was a Swiss follower of Rousseau who emphasized the crucial link between freedom and responsibility in the development of the child. His educational methods stressed the inner dignity of each individual, the need for kindness and encouragement on the part of teachers, and the link among "head, hands, and heart" in all pedagogy.

Rousseau, Jean-Jacques (1712–1778). Rousseau was the source of many of the ideas adopted by British and Continental Romantic poets, philosophers, and artists. He claimed that human beings were essentially good and were corrupted by the selfish, materialistic interests of social organizations. He argued that society was a contract between its members that was always subject to revision, and he advocated a return to nature as a response to the complexities of modern life. His ideas of the noble savage, the freedom of the individual, and the importance of human emotions have proven as widely influential as his autobiographical *Confessions* (1783).

Thoreau, Henry David (1817–1862). Thoreau was a naturalist, author, and social reformer whose two years at Walden Pond became the model for a new kind of connection between humans and the natural world. He eventually became as well known for his idea that "civil disobedience" was a legitimate response to unjust laws. Although he never set forth a consistent philosophy, Thoreau's voluminous writings helped to define the role of wild nature and independent thinking in the development of the individual.

Very, Jones (1813–1880). Transcendentalist poet and mystic remembered for the vagueness but also the intense emotion of his lyric poems. Very described himself as one of God's chosen, and his religious enthusiasm and sensitivity to the world around him helped define one strain of New England Transcendentalism.

Whitman, Walt (1819–1892). Nineteenth-century American poet extraordinaire, Whitman brought a new voice and subject matter into American verse. A largely self-educated laborer and journalist, Whitman virtually invented a loose, free-flowing poetic form that has had a profound influence on subsequent poetry. His *Leaves of Grass* is the often-revised (by Whitman) and, perhaps, single most important volume of poetry in 19th-century America.

Wordsworth, William (1770–1850). Wordsworth was the coauthor, along with Samuel Taylor Coleridge, of *Lyrical Ballads* (1798), a volume of poetry that literally changed the course of English literary history. Wordsworth advocated a return to the language really spoken by human beings and to simple and rustic life in the natural world and the events of ordinary experience as the proper subjects for poetry. He became well known as the best exemplar of Romantic nature poetry in the English language and had a powerful influence on Emerson, Thoreau, and their followers.

Bibliography

Essential Reading:

Albanese, Catherine L. *Corresponding Motion: Transcendental Religion and the New America*. Philadelphia: Temple University Press, 1977. Emphasizes the religious elements of the movement and offers useful links between religious thinking and social history.

Albrecht, Robert, C. *Theodore Parker*. New York: Twayne, 1971. A brief survey in the well-known Twayne series.

Baym, Nina. "The Ann Sisters: Elizabeth Peabody's Millennial Historicism." *American Literary History 3*, no. 1 (1991): 27–45. Baym sets out to rescue Peabody from the "periphery of American Transcendentalism and Romanticism."

Bedell, Madelon. *The Alcotts: Biography of a Family*. New York: Clarkson N. Potter, 1980. A valuable study of the remarkable family behind *Little Women*; a planned second volume was never completed.

Bickman, Martin. "An Overview of American Transcendentalism." www.vcu.edu/engweb/transcendentalism/ideas/definitionbickman.html. Bickman offers a useful survey, especially valuable for its detailed analysis of the historical context of the period.

Boller, Paul F. *American Transcendentalism, 1830–1860: An Intellectual Inquiry*. New York: Putnam, 1974. A comprehensive introduction and survey.

Brooks, Geraldine. "Orpheus at the Plow: The Father of 'Little Women.'" *The New Yorker* (January 10, 2005): 58–65. A wonderful appreciation; Brooks reminds us that Emerson called Alcott "the most extraordinary man and highest genius of the time."

Buell, Lawrence. "Emersonian Anti-Mentoring: From Thoreau to Dickinson and Beyond." *Michigan Quarterly Review 41*, no. 3 (2002): 347–360. Looks at Emerson's attitude toward his role as a mentor and offers important ideas about intellectual influence in general.

———. *The Environmental Imagination: Thoreau, Nature Writing, and the Formation of American Culture*. Cambridge: Harvard University Press, 1995. Exploring the link between environmental writing and ecological awareness, Buell sees Thoreau's imagination as a key source for contemporary ecocentrism and ecocriticism.

————, ed. *Ralph Waldo Emerson: A Collection of Critical Essays.* Englewood Cliffs, NJ: Prentice Hall, 1993. A wide-ranging collection by superb scholars, including Perry Miller, Sacvan Bercovitch, Harold Bloom, and Stanley Cavell.

Conway, Moncure. *Autobiography: Memories and Experiences of Moncure Daniel Conway.* Boston: Elibron Classics, 2006. A reprint edition of Conway's own account of his remarkable life.

Dahlstrand, Frederick C. *Amos Bronson Alcott: An Intellectual Biography.* East Brunswick, NJ: Associated University Presses, 1982. An extended discussion of the development of Alcott's religious thinking, this work also gives a well-rounded picture of his entire life.

D'Entremont, John. *Southern Emancipator, Moncure Conway: The American Years, 1832–1865.* New York: Oxford University Press, 1987. Examines Conway before he went to England, emphasizing his role as a social reformer and abolitionist thinker.

Dickenson, Donna. *Margaret Fuller: Writing a Woman's Life.* New York: St. Martin's Press, 1993. A thoroughly researched feminist biography that sees Fuller as "the intellectual superstar of her sex."

Douglass, Frederick. *Autobiographies: Narrative of the Life of Frederick Douglass, an American Slave*; *My Bondage and My Freedom*; *Life and Times of Frederick Douglass.* Ed. Henry Louis Gates. New York: Library of America, 1994. Part of the carefully produced Library of America series of America's most important authors, this volume includes all three of Douglass's autobiographical volumes in one.

Emerson, Ralph Waldo. *Emerson's Prose and Poetry.* Ed. Joel Porte and Saundra Morris. New York: Norton, 2001. The best single-volume version of crucial texts for understanding Emerson, this Norton Critical Edition also includes letters, contemporary responses, and recent criticism.

Francis, Richard. *Transcendental Utopias: Individual and Community at Brook Farm, Fruitlands, and Walden.* Ithaca: Cornell University Press, 1997. Sees the communities not merely as utopian experiments but as essential outgrowths of Transcendentalist thinking about the relationship between self and society.

Frothingham, Octavius Brooks. *Transcendentalism in New England: A History.* Philadelphia: University of Pennsylvania, 1972. First published by the American Unitarian Association in 1876 and again in 1903, this book remains an essential source for information about the origins, influences, and religious affiliations of the movement.

Fuller, Margaret. *The Essential Margaret Fuller*. Ed. Jeffrey Steele. New Brunswick: Rutgers University Press, 1992. The best collection of Fuller's works in one volume, including her autobiographical and travel writings, *Woman in the Nineteenth Century*, and reviews and essays for the *New York Tribune*.

Grodzins, Dean. *American Heretic: Theodore Parker and Transcendentalism*. Chapel Hill: University of North Carolina Press, 2002. Now considered the standard biography, this excellent study stresses Parker's European influences, his religious radicalism, and his role in the development of the liberal theology of the Transcendentalists.

Gura, Philip F., and Joel Myerson, eds. *Critical Essays on American Transcendentalism*. Boston: G.K. Hall, 1982. From the Transcendentalists to their modern critics, this volume offers a thorough review of the ideas and reception of these thinkers.

Habegger, Alfred. *My Wars Are Laid Away in Books: The Life of Emily Dickinson*. New York: Random House, 2001. Habegger reveals a complex, powerful personality and devotes careful attention to literary analysis of the poems.

Harding, Walter. *The Days of Henry Thoreau*. Princeton: Princeton University Press, 1993. This wonderful biography provides one of the most complete pictures of Thoreau that we have: the author, natural historian, social critic, teacher, disciple of Emerson, the truly self-reliant individual.

Howe, Irving. *The American Newness: Culture and Politics in the Age of Emerson*. Cambridge, MA: Harvard University Press, 1986. Social context offered by a masterful literary historian.

Kaplan, Justin. *Walt Whitman: A Life*. New York: Harper Perennial, 2003. This excellent biography first appeared in a 1980 version. A winner of the National Book Award and Pulitzer Prize, Kaplan gives us a multifaceted Whitman who at once absorbed and reflected the complex democracy he found within himself and without.

Lopez, Michael. *Emerson and Power: Creative Antagonism in the Nineteenth Century*. Dekalb: Northern Illinois University Press, 1996. Links Emerson to Nietzsche, William James, and Henry

Adams and reveals a more pragmatic Transcendentalist in the process.

Mandelker, Ira. *Religion, Society, and Utopia in Nineteenth-Century America*. Amherst: University of Massachusetts Press, 1984. Argues that ideas of utopia were the logical outgrowth of the religious thinking of the time.

Marshall, Megan. *The Peabody Sisters: Three Women Who Ignited American Romanticism*. Boston: Houghton Mifflin, 2005. This carefully researched biography of a family helps to restore the place of three important Transcendentalist sisters.

Martin, Waldo E., Jr. *The Mind of Frederick Douglass*. Chapel Hill: University of North Carolina Press, 1985. An intellectual history of the foremost black American of his time.

McGill, Frederick T., Jr. *Channing of Concord: A Life of William Ellery Channing II*. New Brunswick: Rutgers University Press, 1967. A biography of the eccentric poet and nephew of the theologian whose name he shared.

Mendelsohn, Jack. *Channing, the Reluctant Radical: A Biography*. Boston: Little, Brown, 1971 (Westport, CT: Greenwood, 1980). As the title suggests, Rev. Channing did not relish every aspect of the role he assumed; Mendelsohn makes effective use of Channing's own works, as well as the 1848 *Memoir* by his nephew William E. Channing.

Meyer, Michael. *Several More Lives to Live: Thoreau's Political Reputation in America*. Westport, CT: Greenwood, 1977. Winner of the Ralph Henry Gabriel Prize of the American Studies Association, this work stresses the varying responses to Thoreau's ideas about civil society and civil disobedience.

Myerson, Joel, ed. *Transcendentalism: A Reader*. New York: Oxford University Press, 2000. Outstanding anthology of major texts of the movement.

Newman, Lance. *Our Common Dwelling: Henry Thoreau, Transcendentalism, and the Class Politics of Nature*. New York: Palgrave, 2005. Cautioning against nostalgia for "nature," Newman places Thoreau at the heart of the idea of democratic radicalism.

Peterson, Merrill D. *John Brown: The Legend Revisited*. Charlottesville: University of Virginia Press, 2002. An eminent historian of Jefferson and Lincoln gives us a John Brown who resonates from Bleeding Kansas to the Civil Rights movement of the 1960s.

Porte, Joel. *Representative Man: Ralph Waldo Emerson in His Time.* New York: Oxford University Press, 1978 (Columbia University Press, 1988). Well-researched and well-written biography by a leading scholar of Emerson and his era.

Reynolds, David. *John Brown, Abolitionist: The Man Who Killed Slavery, Sparked the Civil War, and Seeded Civil Rights.* New York: Knopf, 2005. Reversing the tendency to see Brown as a bloodthirsty zealot, Reynolds paints a surprisingly positive picture of the abolitionist and his influence.

Richardson, Robert D. *Thoreau: A Life of the Mind.* Berkeley: University of California Press, 1986. Superbly detailed and wonderfully written, Richardson's is the best recent biography. It offers vivid descriptions of events themselves, from days by the pond to a night in jail, but it also provides rich insights into the intellect as the key to understanding the man.

———. *Emerson: The Mind on Fire.* Berkeley: University of California Press, 1995. Richardson makes excellent use of Emerson's letters and notebooks to flesh out the link between the public and the private man. He balances the cool detachment of Emerson's public persona with the warm family man and friend.

Saxton, Martha. *Louisa May Alcott: A Modern Biography.* New York: Farrar, Straus and Giroux, 1995. First published in 1977, this biography brings the author of *Little Women* into our own world by stressing her tensions with her father, her irreverent ambivalences, and her physical disability later in life.

Thoreau, Henry David. *A Week on the Concord and Merrimack Rivers, Walden; Or, Life in the Woods, The Maine Woods, Cape Cod.* New York: Library of America, 1989. An excellent first source to begin the study of Thoreau's essential texts, except for "Civil Disobedience."

———. *Collected Essays and Poems.* New York: Library of America, 2001. The second primary-source volume needed to fill out a sense of Thoreau's social and political writings, as well as his often-overlooked poems.

Tozer, Steven E., Paul C. Violas, and Guy B. Senese. *School and Society: Historical and Contemporary Perspectives.* New York:

McGraw-Hill, 1995. The relationship between schools and the societies that produced them over the sweep of American history.

Vásquez, Mark G. *Authority and Reform: Religious and Educational Discourses in Nineteenth-Century New England Literature.* Knoxville: University of Tennessee Press, 2003. Unitarian Transcendentalists versus Calvinist Evangelicals or liberals versus conservatives in 19th-century religion and education.

Very, Jones. *The Complete Poems.* Ed. Helen R. Deese. Athens: University of Georgia Press, 1993. This collection of 700 lyrics presents the youthful poet of religious rapture and the later poet of much tamer, less visionary verse.

Whitman, Walt. *Poetry and Prose.* New York: Library of America, 1982. Once again, the Library of America offers an excellent primary-source volume, in this case, a book with which to begin a study of the "barbaric yawp."

"William Ellery Channing." *The Dictionary of Unitarian and Universalist Biography.* www.uua.org/uuhs/duub/articles/williamellerychanning.html. Like many of the useful biographies on this extensive Web site of the Unitarian Universalist Historical Association, this brief survey sets out the essential details of Channing's rich life.

Woodlief, Ann. *The Web of American Transcendentalism.* Virginia Commonwealth University. www.vcu.edu/engweb/transcendentalism/. By far the best single Internet or hypertext resource for the study of the entire movement. Essays by Woodlief and her students (not always as effective), as well as links to a remarkable range of primary and secondary sources, make this an indispensable resource for beginners and more advanced researchers.

Supplementary Reading:

Buell, Lawrence. *Emerson.* Cambridge: Belknap Press, 2003. The best single book on Emerson since Richardson's, Buell's work is more of an intellectual biography than a life story. Not necessarily a book for beginners, this is perhaps the best source for those who want a more advanced understanding of the "Sage of Concord."

———. *Literary Transcendentalism; Style and Vision in the American Renaissance.* Ithaca: Cornell University Press, 1973. Buell carefully analyzes the difficulty of traditional genre criticism in relation to these authors, because they so often broke the boundaries between art and criticism, literature and history, religion and politics.

Cayton, Mary Kupiec. *Emerson's Emergence: Self and Society in the Transformation of New England, 1800–1845.* Chapel Hill: University of North Carolina Press, 1989. Emerson's place in the social history of his early lifetime.

Collison, Gary L. "Theodore Parker." *The Transcendentalists: A Review of Research and Criticism.* Ed. Joel Myerson. New York: MLA, 1984: 216–232. Myerson collects the best bibliographic research sources in these Modern Language Association volumes.

Deese, Helen R. "Emerson from a Feminist Perspective: The Caroline H. Dall Journals." *Postscript 12*, no. 1 (1995): 1–8. Shows how Dall transformed the ideas of Emerson into 19th-century commentary of special interest to feminists.

DeLombard, Jeannine. "'Eye-Witness to the Cruelty': Southern Violence and Northern Testimony in Frederick Douglass's 1845 *Narrative*." *American Literature 73*, no. 2 (2001): 245–275. How can "transcendent poetic vision" fit with the sight of the cruelties of slavery?

De Puy, Harry. "Amos Bronson Alcott: Natural Resource, or 'Consecrated Crank?'" *ATQ 1*, no. 1 (1987): 49–68. Alcott was clearly a bit of both.

Diehl, Joanne Feit. "Emerson, Dickinson, and the Abyss." *ELH 44*, no. 4 (1977): 683–700. Reprinted in Harold Bloom's *Modern Critical Views* volume on Dickinson, this essay argues that "nature" is not always as stable or secure a concept as we might hope.

Garber, Frederick. *Thoreau's Fable of Inscribing.* Princeton: Princeton University Press, 1991. How to find a home through words in a world that seems impermanent and open-ended.

Goodwin, James. "Thoreau and John Brown: Transcendental Politics." *ESQ: A Journal of the American Renaissance 25*, no. 3 (1979): 156–167. Thoreau is not so much social reformer as solitary thinker.

Harris, Kenneth Marc. "Coleridge, Carlyle and Emerson." *Essays in Literature 16*, no. 2 (1989): 263–279. A useful source study of the two most important British influences on Emerson.

Karcher, Caroline L. *The First Woman in the Republic: A Cultural Biography of Lydia Maria Child.* Durham: Duke University Press,

1994. Though it has, no doubt, a hyperbolic title, Karcher's volume nevertheless convinces us of Child's importance as an abolitionist, social reformer, and human rights advocate.

Levin, Jonathan. *The Poetics of Transition: Emerson, Pragmatism, and American Literary Modernism.* Durham: Duke University Press, 1999. Part of the recent move to pull Emerson toward the unstable, if also pragmatic, element in American culture and art.

Loving, Jerome. *Walt Whitman: Song of Himself.* Berkeley: University of California Press, 1999. Carefully researched and full of detail, this is an excellent critical biography of Whitman.

Myerson, Joel, ed. *A Historical Guide to Ralph Waldo Emerson.* New York: Oxford University Press, 2000. A leading scholar of the period brings together valuable essays by others and offers his own introduction and bibliographical essay.

————, ed. *The Cambridge Companion to Henry David Thoreau.* Cambridge: Cambridge University, 1995. Part of an excellent series, Myerson's volume includes wide-ranging essays by Richardson, Gura, Buell, and others, as well as a useful chronology and bibliography.

Robinson, David. "The Legacy of Channing: Culture as a Religious Category in New England Thought." *Harvard Theological Review 74*, no. 2 (1981): 221–239. Channing takes religious thinking far beyond the pulpit.

Rosa, Alfred F. "Alcott and Montessori." *Connecticut Review 3*, no. 1 (1969): 98–103. Links between Alcott's student-centered teaching and the Italian educational reformer who believed that students could learn with less guidance from teachers.

Rosencrans, Jane E. "Transcendentalism for the New Age." www.vcu.edu/engweb/transcendentalism/ideas/rosecrans.html. A convincing sermon delivered to the Unitarian Universalist Church in Glen Allen, Virginia, in 2005.

Schlesinger, Arthur M., Jr. *The American as Reformer.* Cambridge: Harvard University Press, 1950. A thorough, if now slightly dated, analysis of the spirit of reform as the spirit of America; well researched and well written by a masterful historian.

Shealy, Daniel, ed. *Alcott in Her Own Time: A Biographical Chronicle of Her Life, Drawn from Recollections, Interviews, and*

Memoirs by Family, Friends, and Associates. Iowa City: University of Iowa Press, 2005. The title describes this work very well.

Wilson, Eric. *Emerson's Sublime Science.* New York: St. Martin's Press, 1999. An engaging study of Emerson as observer, Wilson's book helps us to appreciate the scientific spirit behind many of Emerson's apparently abstract ideas.

Zwarg, Christina. *Feminist Conversations: Fuller, Emerson, and the Play of Reading.* Ithaca: Cornell University Press, 1995. Conversation was a form of thinking for both Fuller and her close friend Emerson. A valuable contribution to feminist scholarship.